Apples of Gold

A Six-Week Nurturing Program
for Women

Betty Huizenga

Cook Communications

Faithful Woman is an imprint of
Cook Communications Ministries, Colorado Springs, Colorado 80918
Cook Communications, Paris, Ontario
Kingsway Communications, Eastbourne, England

APPLES OF GOLD

Printed in the United States of America.

3 4 5 6 7 8 9 10 Printing/Year 04 03 02 01

Editor: Lorraine Mulligan Davis
Cover design: Andrea Boven
Interior design: Rachael Simpson

Library of Congress Cataloging-in-Publication Data

Huizenga, Betty.
  Apples of gold : a six-week nurturing program for women / Betty Huizenga.
    p.cm.
  Includes bibliographical references.
  ISBN 0-78143-352-5
    1. Christian women—Religious life. 2. Christian women—Conduct of life. I. Title.

BV4527 .H845 2000
267'.43—dc21   99-058924

Here's what women are saying about Apples of Gold . . .

"The lessons were awesome! God knew I needed to be there. My heart overflows with joy."

K.B., Michigan

"In your kitchen I learned about seasoning food. In your living room I reacquainted myself with the seasoning work of the Holy Spirit."

S.O., Michigan

"The program gives value to women who are homemakers and wives. The Bible study and cooking lessons improved my perspective on staying home with children. . . . The program is a good eye-opener and refresher to what is really important: God, husband, children, family, and friends."

D.S, Minnesota

"So many positive things have happened in my life since, and because of, my Apples of Gold summer. Much confidence was gained that went far beyond the kitchen. . . . This was truly a life changing experience!"

L.D., Michigan

"God knew I needed Apples of Gold. It is probably inconceivable to you to know how you and the mentors have touched the lives of Apples of Gold moms!"

L.C., Michigan

"I loved being with older women, finding out how much we have in common, and building relationships with a different generation."

J.R., Michigan

"Apples of Gold makes you focus on what is really important in your life. We discussed subjects I was not familiar with the real meaning of—like submission and purity. It certainly has changed the way I feel about them."

D.H., Minnesota

"Apples of Gold takes the warm atmosphere of the home and teaches how to extend it beyond the immediate family."

Gail Hover Ledbetter
Author, Family Fragrance

To Lee

Thank you for believing in me and Apples of Gold
and for encouraging my heart and spirit.
Thank you for your faithful love to me.
You're the best!
I love you, Sweetheart!

Contents

Acknowledgments

I am thankful to God for instilling the Apples of Gold program in my heart and helping me in its implementation.

I am thankful to Julie Smith, at Chariot Victor Publishing, for believing in the value of this program.

I am thankful for my editor, Lorraine Davis, who has become a precious friend through the process. Her ability to express words and ideas in ways I did not see is a gift to me. She made me think and create. I love you, Lori.

I am thankful for my Apples of Gold partners, the faithful mentors of each class. They make each class a joyful, growing experience for the younger women. I want to thank the mentors who serve faithfully with me in the classes in my home: Carol Berens, Mary De Witt, Marilyn Hontz, Dee Horne, Loraine Maatman, Jinny Nash, and Ruth Slenk. You are so faithful and such a blessing to my heart.

I thank Steve Green for helping me edit the words for each prayer song, and for encouraging my heart with his own kind words.

I thank Janice Faber for taking the music from my heart and tapes and putting it on paper. Janice is an "Applesauce Woman."

I thank Scott Leggett, the talented conductor of our church orchestra, for typesetting the music and preparing it for the book.

I pray this book will challenge our children to continue a tradition of serving the Lord and others, and to be part of the heritage to our "grands": Carly and Lee Huizenga; Tyler, Jason, and Nicolas Hogan; Marcus, Joel, and Gerrit Beltman. I pray they will know that serving the Lord is the highest calling and brings the greatest joy.

Getting Started

Apples of Gold in Shining Silver;
That's what our words should be.
May the glowing of Your Spirit
Reflect, O Lord, in me.

Help me to guard each word I speak;
May only love proceed,
So that what others hear from me, Lord,
Is really what they need.

May all my words be seasoned, Lord,
So richly by Thy grace,
That when others look upon me
They see Your glorious face.

How God Planted the Seeds

Apples of Gold was established in my heart in 1995. I believe the Lord clearly gave me the idea for the program and has blessed it beyond my imagination. It is a unique way to establish relationships with the young women in your church.

It happened this way.

In the spring of 1995, a dear friend asked me to go with her to cooking school at The Greenbrier Resort in White Sulphur Springs, West Virginia. It is a place dear to my heart, a place I had visited several times with my husband. It is surrounded by the Allegheny Mountains, a clear mountain river flows through it, and flowers abound. I couldn't wait for the experience.

My husband and I had just sold our business and retired. He was feeling exuberant, and I was feeling a loss. We had worked together for twelve years, and I missed the people greatly. I also loved the work.

While at The Greenbrier, I took a long walk one afternoon. I asked God what He wanted me to do with my life at this time of change. Actually, I was crying out to Him from my heart. I wanted my life to have value and wanted to serve God. I found a chair on the porch of an old cabin and sat down.

The Lord began to speak to me in my mind—not in a still, small voice, but with a voice of calling. There have been many times in my life when I have felt especially close to God, but never have I felt this kind of call. As I write these words, I can still feel the experience deeply in my heart.

As I sat there, the Lord clearly and directly laid out the entire idea, program, Scriptures, and method for Apples of Gold to me. The verses of Scripture in Titus and Proverbs were brought to my mind, as well as the women who would be my partners in mentoring, and how to begin. I excitedly went to my room and began to write down the ideas that came to me. I had a confidence because I knew God had called me to start this program and He had given me a desire to be obedient.

I wrote a Statement of Purpose, which I gave to my pastor. He encouraged me to go for it.

The program is based on two passages of Scripture:

Proverbs 25:11 says,

A word aptly spoken is like apples of gold in a setting of silver.

What an appropriate picture verse for a program about looking into the Word, about cooking and homemaking. We are to speak the Word in a loving and helpful way. I believe the passage also speaks to our senses. This program needs to be well done. It is to honor the Lord. The visual picture of golden apples surrounded by silver is beautiful. (After five years, I have a lovely collection of gold apples, treasured gifts.)

A friend heard a sermon based on this text. The man, a Messianic Jew, gave the following illustration. He said that when we see a silver bowl from afar, it is beautiful and shiny. We admire it. But it is only when we get closer and peer into the bowl that we see the lovely golden apples, worth far more than the silver. That is how we are to study the Word . . . look inside for the golden nuggets.

Whatever we do in the kingdom of God, we should do the best we can. Yet, we do not need to be an authority on mentoring to be a mentor. We just need to be obedient. We begin with the premise that we are all in process and are learning together with the younger women.

Obedience to the Lord brings peace and joy to our lives. It also brings blessings. Deuteronomy 28:1-14 attests to this fact. Every verse talks about blessings for obedience in various areas of our life. He promises to bless our city and country, our children, our crops, and our livestock. Verse 5 says, "Blessed shall be your basket and your kneading bowl" (NRSVB). I love that verse! The Lord cares about everything we do.

The second passage is Titus 2:3-5. It says,

> *Bid the older women likewise to be reverent in behavior, not to be slan-*
> *derers or slaves to drink. They are to teach what is good, and so train the*
> *young women to love their husbands and children, to be sensible, chaste,*
> *domestic, kind, and submissive to their husbands, that the word of God may*
> *not be discredited (RSV).*

The older women should be examples to the younger women, people to look up to and admire. Then the younger women will listen with respect. Did you notice that the primary qualifications are that the mentor be older and admirable? The passage doesn't say an expert or authority.

The six lessons come from that passage:

1. Kindness
2. Loving Your Husband
3. Loving Your Children
4. Submission
5. Purity
6. Hospitality

I now had the outline and was eager to begin. But how would this all work out? When I returned home, I shared first with my husband, and he was completely sup-portive of the idea. He continues to be an encouragement and helper. He is always interested in new ideas and offers great advice. The day before class, he is in the kitchen with me, helping with advance preparations. It is great!

Another thing on my schedule when I arrived home was a luncheon that my daughter-in-love, Meg, had asked me to hold at our home for her MOPS (Mothers of Preschoolers) committee, about fifteen women. At the luncheon that day, she asked me to share what happened at The Greenbrier. The women were so excited that most of them became the first class, which amazingly began a few weeks later. We were on the way!

I asked several good friends to be mentors, and they graciously agreed to part-ner with me to start Apples of Gold. They are a great source of encouragement and joy.

When the first group "graduated," they were asked to pray about someone to invite to the next class. (Because kitchen space may be limited, this is a good way to handle class sign-up.) It is good for each new woman to know that her friend has prayed for her, and felt led to invite her to the class. It also eliminates the problem of the leaders choosing the next class when so many want to attend.

Apples of Gold Mission Statement

The primary purpose of Apples of Gold is for older women to nurture younger women in the Word of God, the Bible, and to encourage them to obey that Word.

The program is based on the principles taught in Titus 2:3-5, which teach six

ways to enhance our spiritual and personal lives, the lives of our family, and the lives of those around us.

The title of the program comes from Proverbs 25:11, which states:

A word aptly spoken is like apples of gold in a setting of silver.

The secondary purpose of the program is the practical application of these principles:

- Cooking skills
- Relational skills
- Homemaking skills
- Sharing hospitality with others

Take a Look at an Apples of Gold Class

I wish you could visit us before you begin your own Apples of Gold classes. Here's what you would see:

We begin each new series with a luncheon with all the former graduates and the new class members. We call this Applesauce. Each new woman is introduced to the mentors and to the other members so that when class begins the next week, she knows where to come for class, who will be there, and what is expected of her. We ask for a strong commitment, faithful attendance, quality time spent studying the lesson, and a desire to obey the Word of God.

The mentors are present at each meeting, which gives opportunity for the young women to get to know them. Some great friendships have developed among the women.

We meet in a home, which I believe is a very important part of the success of the program. It is a safe haven, it is not church, and the atmosphere encourages conversation. The cook has an easier time if she is familiar with the kitchen. One Apples of Gold program holds classes in several different homes, which I believe is a bit more complicated, but it seems to work just fine.

There is no charge for the program. This, of course, is an option, but I believe if the program can be underwritten, it is best. I know some have the idea that free means unappreciated, but it is my desire to make this program a gift to the busy moms. And it is appreciated! Offering the class at no cost makes it available to all, which is important from a ministry standpoint. It puts everyone on an even plane. It also teaches generosity to all who participate.

We begin at 11:00 A.M. About 10:45 A.M., the women start arriving. They are greeted at the door with a warm welcome and a name tag with their name written in large letters. The first greeting is an amazingly important part of the ministry because it creates a safe, comfortable, and joyous environment. As they walk in, they also receive the recipes and any additional handouts for the day. Some classes give out an Apples of Gold three-ring binder for the extra pages. Ours is green with a gold apple on the front and the words *Apples of Gold* printed on it. A folder with a gold apple stamped on the front will work just fine.

There is much conversation and laughter. The women are enjoying a day out, one made especially for them. They are welcomed, loved, and pampered for two-and-a-half or more hours for six weeks. I am always impressed with how lovely the women look. For them, it is almost like going to a party.

This is what one woman wrote in the photo album I was given at one class:

Apples of Gold was for me a really special time at a rather difficult time in my life. The cooking class was great, and insights in the Bible study were very helpful. However, for me the best part was simply having time for me, and being pampered a bit. God knew that's what I really needed the most.

When the women arrive, I am already busy in the kitchen. Usually I have prepared some treat ahead of time to whet the appetite. It also helps in making conversation. We begin to cook. As I demonstrate the recipes, the women follow along on their own copy of the recipe, adding their own notes as we go.

This is not a basic cooking class, but one that challenges us to try something different and new. It is meant to be a confidence builder, to teach about new seasonings, ingredients, and techniques, and how to use them in new ways.

I am the only one preparing food; the others are watching, much like the cooking school I attended at The Greenbrier. On occasion, we may try to roll pie crust, make egg rolls, or work with a piece of bread dough to get the feel of it.

At times we have prepared Italian, Greek, Chinese, and American food. We have made breakfast, lunch, brunch, and dinner recipes. We talk about working safely with such foods as chicken, and the importance of clean utensils and dishcloths. We prepare food from scratch, and we learn shortcuts. While we cook, the women are asking questions about shopping and menu planning.

This is the time we get to know one another. It is very comfortable, and I believe it is the main reason for the success of this particular program. We are not in a formal setting. It is just great fun!

We cook for forty-five minutes to one hour. It is important to keep to a schedule in order to finish the lesson completely and have adequate time to eat our lunch. After the cooking class, we have our lesson in another room. This gives the cook and helpers time to clean up, finish cooking, and put the food out for lunch.

The mentor for the day is well prepared for her class. Again, she makes everyone comfortable with a warm greeting, a smile, and perhaps a good anecdote. The young women have also prepared ahead, so it is very important that the mentor sticks to the lesson and does not sidetrack too much with things that are not included in the lesson. She may share some personal experiences or stories that apply to the lesson, but it is important to finish the lesson each week. Some sharing is good, but remind the women that they will have time to share and ask questions during lunch. We always want to

focus on what the Bible says on a topic to keep on target.

Sometimes, though, the Holy Spirit is moving in the group, and it is evident that a certain topic needs to be discussed right now. These can be forever moments, and we want to secure them in our hearts.

The lessons are pertinent. They are for the women. They are about how God wants us to live. We are not trying to change the behavior of our spouse, but our own behavior. Our response is our responsibility. When someone is consistently obedient to God, and her family can see that obedience, there are results that are of God's doing.

After the lesson, we have lunch in smaller groups around tables where we eat the food that we saw prepared earlier. I try to set the tables in several different ways. Sometimes the tables are set with good china; other times nothing matches exactly. I use different silverware and plates. Find a way to make the table look lovely with great napkins or flowers. We want everyone to feel that they can entertain with what they have on hand, adding a little creativity.

On each table there are Table Talk questions for discussion. The questions keep everyone involved in the conversation and not feeling left out. It is often at this time the women really share their hearts and changes are made in their lives, with forever results.

Here is an example of how one woman was changed:

It is with great pleasure and privilege that I have an opportunity to tell you what an impact Apples of Gold has had on me and my family. All I need to say is "laundry" and you know the rest of the story. But that was only the beginning. . . . The mentoring sessions were convicting and inspiring. I was truly challenged in many areas, and I am so excited to see what God is going to do in my life. The cooking class was a huge inspiration and help to me. The "dessert" was having a few hours out just for me (something I have never done before). I felt loved, nourished, and pampered, and I had a great time of fellowship. God knew I really needed that.

Early in their marriage, there had been a disagreement about how the laundry should be done (sort of a toothpaste argument). The wife made a comment that if he didn't like the way she did the laundry, he could do it for himself. So he did, for nine years. The day we discussed "Loving Your Husband," one of the Table Talk questions was, *How will I show more love to my husband this week?* She was so convicted about the laundry incident that she left immediately, went home, and did all her husband's laundry. When he arrived home that evening, their daughter, who had helped with Mom's project, greeted Dad at the door and led him into the bedroom to see all his laundered clothing. It was life changing! This had more to do with relationships and problem solving than doing the laundry.

After lunch, everyone is free to leave, but many linger.

The exciting thing is that the program is taken to heart. Women are entertaining who never had a dinner party before. They call me for recipes and menus, and I love that. At Christmas time, Julie had her husband's entire department for dinner. We worked on the menu together. It was a smashing success and a great encouragement to her. Another woman had a Christmas open house. Other women decided to start the tradition of a certain menu for Christmas dinner.

The following quote from a letter gives another testimony to Apples of Gold.

So many positive things have happened in my life since and because of my Apples of Gold summer. Much confidence was gained that went far beyond the kitchen. Apples of Gold was truly a life-changing experience.

New commitments are made to marriages and children, women are convicted about overspending and poor management of their households. The "Purity" lesson is challenging in today's society, as is the "Submission" lesson. Loving children who don't want to obey can be difficult. I believe the lessons help women with these issues.

Many husbands have called and written notes as well. One husband wrote:

I know that this [the letter for the photo album given me] was meant to be written by the Apples of Gold graduates, but I wanted you to hear from a family that has received many benefits from the gift that keeps giving. If you asked Wendy to rate Apples of Gold, she would place it on the list of her most cherished experiences. When she came to your house, Wendy felt that a little bit of heaven reached her as you taught, served, encouraged, mentored, and loved. After each session, she would be so excited about all she had learned watching you cook, and she would pass on the words of wisdom she had received from the mentoring hour.

The ministry has reached not only the heart of my wife, but has given pleasure to our family's dinner table as well. Just this day she continued to share the ministry with our guests as they enjoyed two of the recipes at dinner, which gave Wendy another chance to share your Christian example with them. Once again a blessing grew wings and was passed on to another family.

Thank you for your hours of preparation. . . . You ministered in ways that no one else has to my wife, and my prayer is that you receive as much from this ministry as we have. Thanks for your investment in our Gold Apple.

At the end of each six-week session, we have a dinner with the husbands (or guests). Former participants and their husbands are servers. This is a very special night. Again, the guests are pampered and do not lift a finger (or a plate) all evening. The husbands get a little taste of what their wives have experienced.

All the guests are greeted at the door by a mentor and her husband or guest. We begin with punch and appetizers. It is a time for the women to introduce their husbands or guests to the others.

We have tables set up all over the house. We have to pull in folding chairs, and

some sit on the sofa. What matters is that each table is set as beautifully as we know how. A few flowers can be as lovely as a large bouquet. For us, candles are essential, as are cloth napkins.

While the guests are enjoying the appetizers, we are busy serving the soup. We have an opening prayer and then call everyone to the tables. While our guests are enjoying the soup, we are preparing the salads in the kitchen. Everything is served as individual portions, as in the finest restaurants. We assign someone to care for the water glasses and coffee cups. There is no need to hurry the courses; this is a time for everyone to get acquainted and relax. The main course is presented as beautifully as possible, with garnishes and good color variety. Of course, the dessert must be scrumptious; it is the last impression of the dinner that your guests will take home with them.

We are careful to give good instructions for the kitchen helpers. They need to be able to carry on without the hostess if she is called away for a few minutes. Instructions include a review of the menu, which dishes are for which tables, how the food will be displayed on the dinner plate, which dishes must be hand washed, etc.

After dinner, there is a time of singing and sharing. It is so precious to hear from the women and the men how Apples of Gold has changed their homes, their marriages, their dinner table, and their concept of entertaining others.

The kitchen helpers are called in for a cook's parade.

My husband speaks to the men about doing their part to encourage their wives to put into use the lessons they have learned in Apples of Gold. We close with a time of shared prayer.

Another session of Apples of Gold is over. Lives have been changed. Marriages are revitalized. The younger women shared that they really enjoyed being with the older women; the older women were surprised by the deep feelings they have for the younger women. Families are eating more exciting and healthful food, friendships are made and deepened, and women have been assured that God loves them deeply.

One day one of the graduates dropped over after the class, settled me into a comfy chair, and gave me a foot massage. She brought all the equipment with her. What a wonderful act of servanthood that was! She knew I had been on my feet for many hours. I will never forget that gesture of love to me. Thank you, Susan!

The new graduates often join the ranks of those willing workers who help the ministry continue. Some "Applesauce" women become the kitchen helpers who are so strategic. Others provide child care for the current members, so that they are free to experience Apples of Gold. The graduates are practicing what they have learned.

Starting an Apples of Gold Class

This is a six-week program, with six lessons, plus a celebration dinner with husbands or guests following the six weeks. You may want to extend the program to seven weeks and begin with an introductory luncheon. We have a different mentor for each lesson, one who is well suited to the topic. We also have one mentor who greets each woman when she arrives and makes her feel welcome and special.

If you are interested in starting an Apples of Gold program, call a meeting of interested women, or talk with the women's ministry leader at your church. Begin to pray for guidance and leadership.

These women do not need to be experts, but they must love the Lord, and their lives must reflect the love of Christ and show obedience to Him. They need to be committed to Apples of Gold by attending every week and showing love to the younger women.

The mentors should be women who are compatible with one another, who complement one another. Harmony within the program is essential. Titus says we are to be examples to the younger women.

Call an exploratory meeting with both younger and older women to share the Apples of Gold vision. It is helpful if someone from the group can visit an ongoing class to see firsthand how the program is carried out.

To proceed with the program, you will need a cooking mentor and a place to meet, six mentors to teach the six lessons, and a budget to care for expenses. To make the program available to all women, try to find an underwriter for expenses, or raise the money for the program through a bazaar or yard sale. Churches eager to reach their young moms will put the program into the church budget.

The budget will vary depending on the extent of the cooking. If your budget is limited, you will have to plan your menus carefully, perhaps having soup, salad, and bread for one class, a brunch, a picnic, a tea party, and so on. Each woman will need this *Apples of Gold* book for a study guide, and you will need to print any additional handouts for each class. For more about budgeting for your class, see Funding Apples of Gold, page 22.

You will need a home that will accommodate the size of your group. I recommend the class should have between ten and sixteen participants. It is best if the same home is headquarters for the entire six-week session. The women are sure where to meet, and that home becomes a safe, comfortable haven for the women after the first week. Be sure the home you choose is welcoming and comfortable. The women need to know that they can relax and be themselves.

The Class Schedule

Introductory luncheon (optional) 1-2 hours
Weeks 1-6

> Greeting 10 minutes
> Cooking demonstration 1 hour
> Bible study 50 minutes
> Eat and Table Talk 50 minutes
> Good-byes 10 minutes

Celebration dinner 2-3 hours

The Cooking Mentor[1]

The cooking mentor sets the mood for each class because the cooking segment comes first. The cook should be a woman who is comfortable in the kitchen and a good cook. The cooking mentor makes cooking look easy and fun, someone who can talk with the women about several cooking issues at once. The young women are full of questions about shopping, procedures, recipes, etc., and the questions need to be answered while you are trying to cook! If the cook is frazzled, the young women will feel uncomfortable. If a cooking procedure is not working out, show them how to fix it. It helps them to know that everyone can have a cooking or baking flop from time to time. The important thing is how you deal with it.

The cook must have basic knowledge about food products, food safety, planning menus, and so on. It is best if there is one main cook, but guest cooks provide a fun alternative as well. I have had mentors from other classes in different cities come to cook, as well as a friend and her daughter who are excellent bread bakers. Two friends of mine, a couple who love to cook together, come as guest cooks; they have given the class a new dimension.

If you team teach, you will have to work out the menus with care so there is no repetition. We don't want chicken two weeks in a row. Vary the menus to include beef, pork, chicken, and vegetarian dishes.

As servants of Christ, we want to do the best we can for Him. The younger women have made a good effort to be present, and we want them to be fascinated and excited about the food we make. That will happen naturally when we are prepared and comfortable with the food we are cooking.

It is important to inspire the younger women with your enthusiasm.

If possible, have two helpers (not mentors) in the kitchen to facilitate cooking and to clean up as needed. They also can finish up the cooking and set the food out while the cooking mentor is in the Bible lesson. The women who help me cook also do the dishes after class. They are all Apples of Gold graduates—applesauce

---

[1]See also Help for the Mentors, page 25.

women—who look for any opportunity to get back in class! It is wonderful.

I have a list of tasks ready for the helpers and show them the menu so they know exactly what to do and what my expectations are for them that day. For instance, remove the dirty dishes when I finish a recipe. Stir the sauce on the stove so it doesn't burn while I am teaching something new. Fill the water glasses for lunch, serve the dessert. They also need to know specific things about cleanup, such as which dishes cannot go in the dishwasher, where to put the dishes they wash, where the clean towels and aprons are, and so on.

If you are the cooking mentor, it is your responsibility to plan the menu for each session, print any additional recipes not in the *Apples of Gold* book (or assign someone else to that task), purchase the ingredients for the food, keep track of the receipts, and prep the food in advance. I have a special credit card I use only for Apples of Gold purchases. This helps me with bookkeeping. It you copy recipes from cookbooks or magazines, you'll need to obtain permission to reprint them.

There are six complete menus in this book that are suggestions for the six classes. Most likely, if you are the cook for the class, you are already an excellent cook. Please use whatever menus that are comfortable and easy for you to do. I would always be interested in knowing what menus you use. We cooks love to share recipes. You can reach me at the Apples of Gold Web site: www.applesofgold.org.

Be sure that whatever menus you use, the instructions are clear and any unusual technique is clearly demonstrated in class. The recipes are of no use to the women if they can't go home and have them turn out just as well as in class.

If any women are hesitant to try new recipes, assure them that they can do it. At the beginning of each class, I ask if anyone tried the recipes from last time. Were there any problems? Did your family like the recipe? Did it turn out right?

I once had a problem with explaining the process of making stock. We had to review the recipe several times, and then finally made it one more time. The questions that came up were: Do you brown the meat first? How much seasoning? How many vegetables? How much liquid? Because I believe knowing how to make a good stock is an important part of cooking, I wanted the women to understand the process fully, so we reviewed carefully.

· Planning the Food Around Your Budget

The average budget for a six-week class is $1,000 to 1,200 for twelve participants and six mentors—or $60 to 70 per person. If you need to scale back, you will have to be more creative with your menus. You might also want to figure in the cost of an Apples of Gold three-ring binder or folder for the additional handouts. Class members seem to treasure their notebooks and refer to them often. Perhaps someone can draw a gold apple on the front of a green notebook or write in calligraphy. Be creative. Use yellow or gold paper to print the recipes.

There are more recipes included in each menu than you may need for a class.

The purpose is this: If your budget is limited, you can choose to have soup, salad, and dessert. You could also choose the main course, salad, and bread or dessert.

Another idea is to have a bread-making class, a soup class, a dessert class, and so on. You can also make smaller amounts of food and tell the women that the class is not meant to be a full lunch, but a tasting. This is a common practice used by cooking schools. This idea is especially good for the meat dish, which is your greatest expense. (For instance, in a tasting, a whole chicken breast makes four servings.) The main thing is that the women know what to expect, so they do not go away hungry or disappointed.

Whatever you choose, prepare food with good quality ingredients, using fresh whenever possible. Fix foods that the class does not already make at home. Try not to use prepared mixes on a regular basis. Teach how to make sauces and dressings from ingredients found in the kitchen pantry.

· Sharing Recipes

I have a Master Cook Deluxe (Sierra On-Line, Inc., 1996) program on my computer. Two years ago I put all my recipes on this program, including those of my mom, daughters, relatives, and friends. It allows me to see all my recipes at a glance, choose the ones I want for the week's menu, and print out the copies for class. It is wonderful. It is not an expensive program; it just makes everything so easy. If you do not have time to copy all your recipes at once, begin with the ones that you want to use in class.

When I completed all the recipes, I made a cookbook for each of my daughters for Christmas. I chose a large loose-leaf notebook, so we can add to it. My friend painted white checks on the black notebook, and added clusters of red cherries. Inside the cover, she painted a verse that I asked for. The girls were just thrilled; it is part of their heritage. Since that time, I have given similar books to very special brides in my life. I can print the entire book with the press of a single button, every recipe in its category. I print on paper that has reinforced holes already punched. All I have to add is section pages in the notebook, and I have a great gift!

· Preparation and Presentation

The night before class, I measure ingredients into small, clear Pyrex dishes and cover them with plastic wrap. I put all the ingredients for each recipe on a tray with a copy of the recipe. I line the trays up on the counter in order, making sure all the ingredients are on the tray at the time the class begins. This saves time and confusion.

Some dishes are prepared completely ahead of time, and I prepare just a small sampling in class. For instance, you may need two cakes for a class, depending on the size of your class. In that case, I make one ahead, and one in class. The same is true for each recipe.

It is important to show or explain every step of the recipe. We cannot assume that the women know how to do the procedure. For instance, a recipe may include roasted red peppers. You will need to roast a red pepper in class, or chop garlic, for example. When you are cutting an onion or chopping garlic, take the time to explain about different types of knives, about care of knives, sharpening of knives (do a quick illustration), and storing knives. Take your recipes apart, ingredient by ingredient, and ask yourself: "How can I explain clearly to the women what to do?" Encourage questions, and ask the women if they understand.

The women should have their recipes and a pen in hand. They will write down everything they don't understand and any tips you give.

· Table Settings

You will need tables for lunch to accommodate four to six persons. Folding tables work just fine. Use any rooms you have available. My friend Nancy uses her bed-room for one of the tables. It is wonderful and fun. I have had women sitting on pillows on the floor around my large sofa table. It looked very pretty.

Set the tables in a variety of ways, and as prettily as you can. If you are too busy with the food preparation, ask a creative friend or one of the mentors who is not teaching that week to take over the decorations. It does not need to be elaborate, just special in some way. Even one flower in a vase makes a great difference.

Remember that some women were never taught the proper way to set a table. Even the table settings are part of the Apples of Gold program. Show different ways to fold napkins, have the proper flatware for your menu (such as soup spoons or dessert forks). I set one place setting each week on the countertop in the kitchen, explain what each item is for, and then display the food after cooking. This is a real confidence builder for the women, who may not know the proper way to set a table or display a plate of food. It is a good idea to recommend a good etiquette book.

Show them how to mix and match dishes, silverware, and glasses. They may not have a large matched set of dishes. A table setting can be pulled together with nap-kins and flowers. Everything you do to help them with this is a confidence builder and encourages them that they can show hospitality in their own homes.

If your menu has a theme, you can decorate accordingly. Here are some ideas:

· Loving Your Husband:

Decorate each table with three framed wedding pictures (brought by different women) facing outward and draped with white curling ribbon in a sea of wedding confetti.

· Italian Meal:

Use red-and-white checked tablecloths and/or napkins. Paper will do if you do not have a cloth set. Purchase a box of tubular pasta and use pasta as straws. Put a

flower in a Perrier bottle or similar bottle. Remind the women that candles are wonderful, but only at night.

· Loving Your Children:

A crown cake makes a memorable centerpiece. If you would like to put one on each table, mentors or Applesauce Women might help prepare the many cakes needed. To make the cake, bake a double-layer cake, frost cake, then frost eight mini-size, pointed ice-cream cones and roll them in sprinkles. Arrange cones, point up, around edge of cake top. Put a maraschino cherry on the point of each cone. Wrap a wide ribbon (approximately three inches) around cake. Using frosting for glue, decorate the ribbon with candy. Put M & Ms or sprinkles over the top. It is great! Put a sticker under one plate at each table. The winner takes the cake home.

Throughout the lesson on loving children, one mentor, Mary, uses the illustration of watering our children with our love.

As a memento, she makes a watering can with flowers in it for each woman. It is put at each woman's place at the table. The watering cans were purchased at a local dollar store, the flowers came from her yard. It takes some work, but the rewards are great. Whenever the women spy those watering cans, they will remember that their children are unique seeds that God has entrusted to them to water with love.

As you use a special item or serving piece, assure the women they don't need everything at once. Perhaps they can request a pretty platter or tablecloth as a birthday or Christmas gift. Or they might pick out a practical cookbook to ask for. Each week, have several displayed. Four of my favorites are listed after the menus.

The Teaching Mentor

You will need six teaching mentors, one for each lesson. These women must love the Lord and reflect His love in their lives. They must be caring and loving, good listeners, and faithful to the ministry of Apples of Gold. It is important that all mentors attend each meeting of the six-week session and the dinner for members and spouses held at the end of the program.

Each woman must be qualified to speak about her assigned topic. She must have a good marriage, live a pure life, be hospitable, and so on. It is helpful if she adds personal anecdotes to her lesson to personalize it. For instance, if a woman has struggled with submission in her marriage and she and her husband have successfully worked it out, she will have good advice and lessons to teach.

It is the job of the teaching mentor to keep the lesson on target, both the topic and the schedule. Some interaction is wonderful, but it is also needful to finish each lesson in one week. The women have worked on their questions and they should have a time to share their answers. Since there may not be time to review each and every question, the mentor should prioritize ahead of time what questions she will summarize and which she will solicit answers for. The Scripture should also be read in class, or summarized, if it is a long passage. The mentor should plan all this in advance.

The mentor should note all the numbered apple symbols throughout the lesson. They refer to the optional teaching tips at the end of the lesson. The section is identified by this heading:

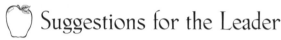

Suggestions for the Leader

Fortunately, there is additional time for discussion around the luncheon table after the lesson. You may also want to sing a praise chorus or use one of the prayer songs included in this book.

There are times, however, when a topic brings an unexpected discussion that is necessary to talk out. The mentors need to be sensitive to the leading of the Holy Spirit.

Sometimes the mentor personalizes the lesson with a small gift. For instance, one mentor gave each woman a small bottle of seasoned salt that was her own recipe. She used the illustration that we can choose to live a bland, unseasoned life, or one richly seasoned with the Word of God.

We want to personalize the lessons and make the women feel special and understood. We want the women to remember the lessons and incorporate them into their lives. Remember, every detail is important! Every person is important!

Table Talk

Remember that the young women do so much for their families every day that they truly appreciate anything done for them. Make this their special time. The mentors are present to serve the younger women. Most of the participants are busy moms, used to jumping up from the table to serve their families. We want them to sit, relax, and feel like princesses for a few hours. If mentors need help, ask for volunteers who are not currently in the program.

You'll need one teaching mentor per table. If you serve buffet style, the mentors should be first in line. This allows them to find their places at the table and be ready to greet the first younger woman to the table.

When mentors go last, the women are already in discussion about other topics, and it can be hard to get to the Table Talk questions. The women also may forget to leave places at the table for the mentor.

It is also important that the mentors stay at their places and are not getting up and down. (The kitchen helpers should be replenishing drinks, etc., so that everyone can stay seated.) Mentors should keep the discussion on target and not let the discussion drift to mundane, everyday topics, or let cliques form. It is easy for someone to feel left out. See to it that each person has the opportunity to share her opinion. It is important to use all the time in a useful manner to help the women to grow in Christ. Life-changing things happen at the lunch table every single week!

Let the women feel free to leave at the agreed end time of class. However, it is important that they also are welcome to linger for a few extra minutes, if they want to discuss something with a mentor. Let them have privacy and a quiet place to talk.

The same woman who is greeter should be at the door to say good-bye at the end of class. She will be able to tell if a woman seems troubled about anything as she leaves, and perhaps make a time to call and check on her later in the week.

In one class, one mentor is the official greeter. She believes God called her to do that job. She does not teach a lesson; she is the greeter. This woman has a sensitive heart and a bold spirit to share Christ. She knows the women and can sense if they need something extra that week.

The mentors need to be available for one-on-one discussion with the young women, as needed. Some women may ask you to lunch or to their homes to discuss a problem or need that they have. That is true success.

Apples of Gold is beneficial to the mentor as well as to the mentoree. It has brought a joy and dimension to my life I have never had before. How wonderful it is to have this lovely bouquet of young women friends in my life. They have tremendous love to give, and the mentors are the recipients of that love.

The younger women also have a lot to teach the mentors. They help us to understand not only them but our own grown children. They keep us thinking young, they make us laugh and cry. They are true friends. We learn from one another and grow together. Don't miss this incredible opportunity in your life.

Funding Apples of Gold

The average budget for a six-week class is $1,000 to 1,200 for eighteen people. Here are some possible ways to fund the program:

• Find a person or persons who will underwrite the entire program.

• Have mentors pay for the food.

• Have your church put Apples of Gold into the church budget as a part of the women's ministry.

• Have a few fund-raisers, such as yard sales or pancake breakfasts.

• Have participants purchase their own books.

• Have participants pay a weekly fee (which, for a complete meal plus program, could be about $7 a week). However, this option might keep someone from attending, so I would use this only as a last resort.

Here are some possible ways to keep costs low:

• Since the main expense is the food, you can limit the menu to:

—soup, salad, and dessert

—entree, salad, and bread or dessert

—bread-making class, dessert class, or soup class
• Make all the dishes, but only have a tasting of the main course.
• Economize on extras, such as having only a single flower in a vase on each table, rather than small arrangements.

However, your heart may be so filled with love for these women that you serve them the very best. One group traditionally serves a filet mignon six-course dinner for the final night with the spouses.

If you are in a small church, or for any reason the cost of the cooking class is a burden, the classes can be made easier by a simplified menu. Eliminating the cooking, however, would be a mistake, because it is what makes this program unique. Be as creative as you can with your costs.

In one class the church really took hold of the program. The women's ministry of the church holds an annual yard sale, and they put Apples of Gold into their budget. We kept records of costs for each luncheon and for study materials, and they came up with a budget based on these costs. This is an ideal solution. In another class, a host underwrites the cost as part of her ministry in Christ's name to the younger women.

A Personal Note

When I was a young mother, I really needed a spiritual mentor. I didn't know that was what I needed until we moved to a new city and home. We found a church where people really enjoyed being children of God. Their lives reflected Christ; I knew mine didn't. God sent some wonderful friends to us there. One couple in the church invited our family to dinner at their home after church.

It seemed to be their custom to invite new families along with other members of the church. I admired them immediately. Their home was so warm, beautiful, and comfortable. I remember looking around at the lovely way everything was displayed, the cozy room arrangements, and the delicious dinner. To this day, though we live far away and don't see one another, my memories are clear of that lovely occasion.

The day we moved in, my now dear friend Orletta came to the house. She invited me to a Bible study in her home where she began modeling for me what a woman of God looks like. She was knowledgeable and bold to speak the truth. For the first time, I was really digging into the Word and trying to apply the Word to my life. I struggled with the issue of obedience. I did my own study on every passage I could find about obedience. It ministered to my needy heart. Our times with Jack and Orletta are always treasured.

Another neighbor, Brenda, and I had long talks about the Lord over cups of spiced tea. Her sweet spirit always ministered to my heart. We now visit in person only occasionally, but thanks to e-mail, we can stay in touch.

What kind of relationship are you willing to have with your neighbors and

friends? Not only can lifetime friendships be built, but God can use us to share His love so we can share eternity together! My friends taught me that our homes belong to God and that sharing His home with others is very important.

If you are interested in a class like Apples of Gold, pray and ask the Lord to show you how you can help make it happen in your neighborhood or church. If you desire to serve the Lord following the Titus passage and do not have a program nearby, you can study the lessons on your own and put them into practice in your life.

One friend started an Apples of Gold class in her neighborhood. When the class was over, a father of one of the young women made plaques for each mentor. He was so thankful that these women had given the gift of Apples of Gold to his daughter. The daughter took hold of the lessons taught and learned new cooking skills that inspired her in her marriage. Her father had been praying for someone to influence his daughter in this very way! When I met Jill recently, she gave me one of her father's plaques. It is very special to me. This class is truly reaching the neighborhood for Christ. It makes a new neighborhood a close-knit group of friends.

This same group of mentors had a class that included several of their daughters. They were able to talk over God's Word with their grown daughters, and help one another grow in Christ. What a wonderful opportunity!

In Minneapolis, eighty-seven-year-old Evie Young is the guest cook. She twice cooked for the king of Sweden; now she cooks for daughters of the King of Heaven. This beautiful, vivacious Swedish woman inspires the women with her love for life and cooking. Her strong hands knead Swedish rye bread, roll Swedish meatballs, and make delicate butter cookies.

Evie was a schoolteacher and owned a bowling alley to which her family added a restaurant. Then she ran the cafeteria at Gustavus Adolphus College in St. Peter, Minnesota. There she cooked for up to two thousand students three times a day for thirty-one years. In the summertime, she cooked for seven hundred campers three times a day. The new dining room at Gustavus Adolphus is now named the Evelyn Young Dining Room.

Evie will stay young at heart forever because she is interested in loving and serving others. Her life is full and joyous. If you ask her how she is, she answers, "Just fabulous, honey. Just fabulous." She inspires me with her positive attitude!

This spring, 1999, my husband took me back for a few wonderful days at The Greenbrier. We walked back to the cabin where the inspiration for Apples of Gold first came to me, and the chair was still there. As I sat down, my heart was filled with joy because of the way the Lord is blessing this program—His idea! I am so thankful for His pursuit of my obedience, and the great encouragement His Spirit continues to be for Apples of Gold. I was only thinking of Holland, Michigan, and the women in my home church. God had a bigger idea.

I encourage you to start an Apples of Gold program wherever you think it can be helpful. If I can be of help to you, please contact me at www.applesofgold.org.

Help for the Mentors

Planning the Menu

Start planning your menus well ahead of class time. Choosing the foods to prepare is always the hardest part for me because I want to teach the young women so many things. So I need to focus on menus that work well for me, and then stick to them. Once I have chosen and printed the menus, I have a great task accomplished.

Ideas to Consider When Planning Your Menu:

• Set up a budget. Consider how much money you have to spend in total, then plan accordingly. In order to have a more elaborate menu one week, you may choose to have a lighter menu another week, such as soup, salad, and dessert.

Plan menus for various occasions: family dinners, dinners for guests, a brunch. I like to do an Italian day, a Chinese day, a Sunday brunch, a picnic, and so on.

• Do not overextend yourself. If you are a frazzled cook, the younger women will feel it and become discouraged. Prepare foods that you have prepared before, so you are comfortable.

• Shop early for the supplies and groceries you will need. Do you have enough ice? Is there ample room in your refrigerator and freezer for the food you have planned? Look at every recipe, check for ingredients, and make good lists.

• Set the tables the day before. It allows you time to be sure that everything you need is ready—clean tablecloths, polished silver, and so on. Have fun with that; make it enjoyable and beautiful.

Put the recipes on your counter, and consider the order in which you will prepare them in class. If a food needs an hour of baking, make it first, to assure it will be ready to eat. Measure the ingredients for each recipe you will make in class. I like to use separate trays for each recipe. I put the recipe with all its ingredients on one tray so I am not searching for the vanilla during class. This method also helps to keep the pace. Remember not to run overtime! Every part of the class is important.

If there is not enough time in class to show a complete recipe or if something has to cook or bake for a longer time, prepare one recipe the day before and one in class.

Choose the plates on which you will display the food. Does the platter enhance the color of your food? Gather the serving pieces. Put them in the kitchen in a convenient place.

Choose foods appropriate for the season of your class. A summer class will appreciate lighter foods, a cold soup, a delicious main-dish salad, a tall glass of

homemade lemonade. A winter class will love hearty soups with meat and winter vegetables.

Be sure that the recipes in your menu have a variety of tastes, textures, and colors. Think about the completed meal on a plate; does it have life to it, or is everything the same? Add garnishes for color, where needed.

When the cooking segment is over, you will have only fifty minutes to have all the food ready for the meal. Planning is vital; so is a helper or two.

Six menus are included in this book. They have instructions for preparation as well. These menus should not limit your creativity. Feel free to prepare foods you love.

Grand Finale Dinner with Spouses or Friends

This should be as special a dinner as you can dream up. I have chosen not to give a menu for this meal because I believe every good cook has a wonderful, favorite meal. But here are some suggestions for the evening:

Have some delicious, but light, appetizers and a great punch ready when guests arrive. Be sure all guests are greeted and given a name tag.

After half an hour, have your helpers for the evening serve a delicious, perhaps creamy, soup. Someone will offer the prayer before the group is seated. Have soup already in bowls on the table when guests sit down.

While guests are eating the soup, prepare the salad, and dish it out onto salad plates. Have servers remove the soup bowls. *Be sure that guests stay seated and do not help.*

While guests are eating salad, prepare the dinner plates with the main course. Remove salad plates, and serve dinner. Now you will have a short breather while the guests are eating the main course. Take the time to clean up the kitchen a bit and load the dishwasher with the first load.

Now have servers take orders for coffee and tea. Have both ready with cream and sugar on the tray.

Prepare desserts, and serve with coffee and tea. Keep the water glasses filled!

When the time is right, have guests leave the tables so you can do a quick cleanup. Tell guests where rest rooms are, and give them a short break. If you give a long break, guests will think the party is over and begin to leave. *The best is yet to come!*

Have guests gather together in the living room or family room, or wherever you can all be together. It is good to sing a few choruses, with or without accompaniment. This time will prepare the way for sharing. Ask if anyone has something to share about their experience with Apples of Gold. After a time of sharing, have a husband of one of the mentors say a few words to the group, perhaps encouraging the husbands to support their wives and help with hospitality in their own homes.

Close the night with a time of shared prayer.

It is my deepest prayer for you that this will be a night of great blessing and reward! May God bless you as you share your servant hearts with young women. Before long, they will be sharing your rich gift to them with others, and the gift continues!

Bon appétit!

"... Train the young women to love their husbands and children, to be sensible, chaste, domestic, kind, and submissive to their husbands, that the word of God may not be discredited." Titus 2:3–5 (RSV)

Lesson One

Kindness

Give me a heart of kindness, Lord.
Cause my eyes to see.
The needs of those around me,
The ones you sent to me.

Give me a heart of kindness, Lord,
For those who are in need,
That they may see Your face in mine
And on Your goodness feed.
—B.H.

Apple Seeds

Set the mood by singing "Give Me a Heart of Kindness, Lord" (music on p. 139).

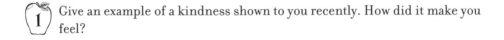 Give an example of a kindness shown to you recently. How did it make you feel?

Give an example of a kindness shown by you recently. How did it make you feel?

Apple Blossoms

In Titus 2:3-5, our foundational passage for Apples of Gold, kindness is an attribute mentioned for older women to teach younger women. This fruit of the Spirit is foundational for the rest of the passage. If we are not kind, how can we have a wonderful marriage, or properly love our children, submit to others, or have the consistent moral excellence which is purity? And certainly a household that does not display kindness would not feel comfortable or hospitable to others.

2️⃣ A good friend owns a food business in Michigan. One winter he knew we were entertaining for a week a group of young men with special needs. One morning I received a phone call from his secretary. She told me to expect a package that morning. Our friend sent two boxes of frozen food in dry ice to us in Florida all the way from Michigan. He was a long-distance host to our guests. It was a blessing!

I have been able to pass on that blessing. One day my friend Dee forgot she was having guests for dinner until late afternoon. We had been out to lunch and shopping that day and on the way home, she remembered the dinner. She went home and got the house and table ready. I went home and made dinner and sneaked it through the back door. Her guests never knew the difference. It made a wonderful memory for us, and she has returned the favor of hospitality to me countless times more. We delight in sharing food gifts with one another when we have guests.

When friends have shown gifts of kindness to me over the years, it makes me want to reciprocate kindness to them, and others. Kindness blesses the giver as well as the receiver.

Kindness is a character quality that is easy to recognize, yet hard to define. One way to describe it is "showing personal care and concern in meeting the needs of others."

What's your mental picture of a kind person? A grandmother tenderly comforting a child? In reality, kindness can be as unique and varied as the ways a caring heart can meet the needs of others.

If we desire to be like Christ, we must ask Him to develop kindness in us. It begins by thinking about God's kindness to us, His generous grace to us, His acceptance and forgiveness of us. It is God's kindness, not our goodness, that allows us to come to Him.

Write out Romans 2:4:

Kindness might be described as a willingness to go the extra mile. It is an attitude, not just actions.

Write your own description of kindness:

Write out Psalm 103:13:

$\widehat{3}$ What does it mean to be compassionate? How is compassion different from kindness? How do they work together?

Kindness is an attitude and a decision. Our decision to be kind and tenderhearted can make a tremendous difference in our lives, our homes, our friendships, our church, or our community. We need the Lord's help to keep an attitude of kindness. Because it is His will for us to be kind, we can be assured He will answer our prayers for help in demonstrating kindness.

Read 1 Kings 17:7-16. The prophet Elijah knocked at the widow's door, asking for kindness and offering a miracle in return. By asking the widow to feed him first out of her meager provisions, what was Elijah requiring of her?

$\widehat{4}$ Many times, demonstrating kindness (meeting the needs of others) takes faith that God will meet our needs. When have you given to others when you thought you had nothing to give? How did God meet your need?

A great pioneer missionary set out on the strength of one final paycheck. Later he would say, "God's work, done in God's way, never lacks God's supply."

Philippians 4:6-7 says, "Don't worry about anything; instead, pray about everything; tell God your needs and don't forget to thank him for his answers. If you do this you will experience God's peace, which is far more wonderful than the human mind can understand. His peace will keep your thoughts and your hearts quiet and at rest as you trust in Christ Jesus" (TLB).

List three steps outlined in this verse for appropriating God's peace in times of need.

1.

2.

3.

⑤ In order to thank God for His past answers, those answers need to be fresh in your mind! It's helpful to record them as they come. Begin by listing a few here:

Read 1 Thessalonians 5:15. What makes this the hardest kind of kindness to offer?

Have you experienced times when it has been difficult to be kind to someone? How did you resolve it?

⑥ Relationships can be difficult for many reasons. Sometimes it is difficult to show kindness and compassion to those who are different from us, or with whom we are uncomfortable: the poor, the rich, the emotionally or mentally impaired, those with personalities different from ours. I hope that part of your answer was to pray about it. Prayer may or may not change the difficult situation with someone, but prayer can change your heart. How would thanking God for His past kindness to you help the situation?

The Bible says, "Out of the overflow of the heart the mouth speaks" (Matt. 12:34). Today we say, "What is down in the well comes up in the bucket."

If your heart is a well, what would each of these hearts yield?

Angry Heart ————▶_____Words
Dirty Heart ————▶_____Words
Pessimistic Heart ————▶_____Words
Agitated Heart ————▶_____Words
Insecure Heart ————▶_____Words
Bitter Heart ————▶_____Words
Happy Heart ————▶_____Words
Peaceful Heart ————▶_____Words
Pure Heart ————▶_____Words
Contented Heart ————▶_____Words
Gentle Heart ————▶_____Words
Hopeful Heart ————▶_____Words

The way we approach a situation shows our inward heart! Proverbs 14:30 says, "A heart at peace gives life to the body." We have that verse painted over our living-room window. Unkindness among people causes stress to the family and to the body. Though some say, "Peace at all costs," Romans 12:18 shows God's wisdom when it says, "If it is possible, as far as it depends on you, live at peace with everyone."

Underline the attitudes or emotions that hinder kindness.

Star those that encourage kindness to difficult people. Choose one to work on in a difficult relationship.

BITTERNESS	SELFISHNESS
COMPETITION	COMPARISONS
EMPATHY	DISDAIN
DESIRE FOR REVENGE	CARING
ATTACHING LABELS	LAZINESS
PLACING OTHERS ABOVE SELF	TEACHABLE SPIRIT
PRIDE	FEELING THREATENED
LISTENING	PATIENCE
HUMILITY	

Try to get to know the people who are difficult in your life. Try to understand what their needs or insecurities are, what causes them to act the way they do toward you. Communicate with them, tell them you want things to be different, and ask how that can happen.

Summarize the advice given in the following verses:

Nehemiah 9:17

2 Timothy 2:24

1 Thessalonians 5:15

The Lord does not allow us to pick and choose those to whom we will be kind. Everyone is every one! Notice also that 1 Thessalonians 5:15 says "try to be kind. . . ." God knows it can be difficult for us at times, and others may not accept our kindness.

⑦ It is difficult to love our enemies, especially if they are determined to bring harm to us. Loving them is the choice, because it is the only way to bring a positive reaction to the situation. Is there anyone hard for you to love? Pray for him or her. It is difficult not to care for someone if you are praying for that person on a regular basis. Trust the Lord to change your relationship with that person.

Once we have an attitude of kindness, we must find ways to meet the needs of others—with words and actions.

Jesus was a wonderful example of kind words. In 1 Peter 2:22 we read, "He committed no sin and no deceit was found in his mouth." Jesus' words were truth laced with grace.

Listen to some of the kind words of Jesus. Read them aloud:

• "Come to me, all you who are weary and burdened, and I will give you rest." (Matt. 11:28)

• "Peace I leave with you; my peace I give you." (John 14:27)

• "Do not let your hearts be troubled. Trust in God; trust also in me." (John 14:1)

• "Let the little children come to me, and do not hinder them, for the kingdom of heaven belongs to such as these." (Matt. 19:14)

Jesus didn't just tell people what they wanted to hear. Many times He told them what they needed to hear. He met their deeper needs. He was motivated by love. Read aloud these examples of the tough love of Jesus:

• "I tell you the truth, no one can see the kingdom of God unless he is born again." (John 3:3)

• "Woman, where are they? Has no one condemned you? . . . Then neither do I condemn you. . . . Go now and leave your life of sin." (John 8:10-11)

• "You diligently study the Scriptures because you think that by them you possess eternal life. These are the Scriptures that testify about me, yet you refuse to come to me to have life." (John 5:39-40)

Jesus was able to say hard things in love because He spoke with discernment. According to Proverbs 21:23 and Psalm 141:3, how does this work?

Choice Fruit

Galatians 5:22 says that one of the fruits of the Spirit is kindness. What are some practical ways to show kindness to . . .

• Family

(My friend Jean says, "Let love spill out the door." What wonderful advice! A young mom I know and her children say a blessing to one another in the morning before the children leave for school. They say, "May the Lord protect and keep you today.")

• Friends

(Find a need and fill it. Give others what they need most. Express your appreciation.)

• Church

(One church asks its members not to talk with friends after services until they have spoken with someone they don't know. It is easy to talk with our friends and acquaintances, but it is more important that we welcome a visitor.)

• Neighbors

(In Acts 1:8, Jesus told His followers they would be His witnesses in Jerusalem—right in their own backyard!)

We want to be like our Heavenly Father and respond to others the way He responds to us. The Golden Rule says, "Do to others what you would have them to do to you." (Matt. 7:12). That means being slow to anger and abounding in love (Ex. 34:6). Remember that anger is an emotion; kindness is a decision. We want to treat others as Christ treats us.

Prayer

Lord Jesus, give me a heart full of kindness. Help me to be sympathetic and compassionate to those around me. May my loved ones feel my sweetness and tenderness for them. Keep my tongue from evil and my lips from speaking guile.

Thank You, Lord, for being such a perfect example of kindness and compassion to me, for being tenderhearted to me and forgiving me over and over again, and for not remembering my sinful words and deeds after I confess them to You and ask for forgiveness. Lord, I want to be obedient to the admonitions from Your Word. Amen.

"May the words of my mouth and the meditation of my heart be pleasing in your sight, O Lord , my Rock and my Redeemer." Psalm 19:14

8 *Preparing for Next Week's Lesson:* The Loving Your Husband study suggests reading through Song of Solomon a little each day throughout the next week.

 # Suggestions for the Leader

1 If time permits, have a few participants share their Apple Seeds.

2 I began with examples of kindness demonstrated in my life that were passed along. You may substitute an enticing description of a woman who demonstrated kindness in your own life—and the wonderful results.

3 Bring out the fact that where kindness seeks to meet needs, compassion involves identifying and healing hurts.

Offer an example of a time when you had to depend on God to give through you because, like the widow at Zarephath, you had nothing to give.

 It might be helpful to show the group some methods of keeping a record of God's answers. One might be a notepad that can be kept handy in a purse. A more elaborate version is a pretty file box where answers are recorded on separate index cards. Extra file cards can be stored in your purse so that new ideas aren't lost. Some families review the contents of such boxes during times of discouragement, as well as at Thanksgiving or New Year's dinner.

Be prepared with examples of ways God's kindness to you has been your strength.

Working to improve relationships with difficult people can be an overwhelming process. Assure the participants that you or the other mentors are available to offer guidance.

Because some of your participants may do their lessons just before the next session, point out that this week they are asked to read Song of Solomon throughout the week.

Show Random Acts of Kindness

Write a note of appreciation to someone special.

Write thank-you notes to your pastor and church staff.

Do something special for your child or husband.

Bake something for a busy mom or a sick neighbor.

Give a gift to someone you don't know but see often (such as a Christmas gift to the person at the McDonald's window).

Do something for your mother and mother-in-law.

Plant a tree in your neighborhood.

Put an extra shopping cart back in its appointed place in the parking lot.

Write a note to the boss of someone who has helped you, thanking him or her for having such a great employee.

When someone tries to merge into your lane, smile and wave while you let the car in.

If there is a garden you enjoy, let the owner know how much pleasure it gives you.

Laugh aloud often and share your smile generously.

Appreciate yourself as a random act of kindness.

Think of your own random acts of kindness.

Enjoy!

Be Kind to Yourself

It is also important to show kindness to yourself. You can do that by pampering yourself from time to time with a new book to read, a luxurious bath, a manicure, a new hairstyle, a walk alone on the beach, or a shopping trip. (Even a window-shopping trip can be therapeutic!)

Even though bouts of pampering can be difficult and make you feel guilty, they are really necessary if you are to be helpful and loving to others.

What would be a wonderful gift from you to you? Do it!

You need to pamper your emotions as well. Moms especially can be really hard on themselves. You need time to pray and study Scripture, to talk with the Lord about anything that is hurting you. Sometimes you need to talk with a good friend. Neglecting your own emotions hurts those around you.

Start today. Make time for yourself—and enjoy it!

". . . Train the young women to love their husbands and children, to be sensible, chaste, domestic, kind, and submissive to their husbands, that the word of God may not be discredited." Titus 2:3-5 (RSV)

Lesson Two

Loving Your Husband

Choose Love
I want to choose love every day.
In everything, in all I do and say
Through days of joy and waters deep,
Help me my sacred vows to keep.
To love, honor, and obey,
Help me to choose love every day.
Your example, Lord, is true,
Help me each day to follow You.
—B.H.

Apple Seeds

Set the mood by singing "Choose Love" (music on p. 140).

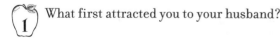 What first attracted you to your husband?

What was the first thing your husband noticed about you? Are those things still important?

Apple Blossoms

Once a pastor was giving a children's sermon. He asked, "What's gray and furry and hops about in the forest?" A boy tentatively raised his hand to say, "I know the answer is Jesus, but it sure sounds like a squirrel to me!"

In the same way, it's easy to guess the "right" answer to the following question, but what is the "real" answer? Here's the question: How would you order these relationships in your life?

GOD	CHILDREN	HUSBAND

Though the "real" answer is often Children, Husband, God, the "right" answer is: God, Husband, Children. Your relationship with God must be the most important relationship in your life. Everything you do hinges on this relationship—the decisions you make, the reactions you have to circumstances, the way you relate to others, your sense of joy and peace. Everything! Your relationship with God is for time and eternity.

Furthermore, your relationship with the Lord affects all the other relationships in your life. We see in 1 John 4:7-8: "Dear Friends, let us love one another, for love comes from God. Everyone who loves has been born of God and knows God. Whoever does not love does not know God, because God is love."

Write out Matthew 6:33:

Before we can understand, desire, and fulfill true love in our marriage, we need to have a right relationship with the Lord.

What does a right relationship with the Lord mean?

Why is it important?

2) Having a right relationship with the Lord is important because God is the only one who can meet your ultimate needs. Your spouse or friends cannot fill the "hole in your soul." The issues of self-worth, loneliness, strength in the hard times, freedom from fear, and joy are resolved only by a right relationship with the Lord.

When Christ is your first love, He enhances your marriage by helping you understand one another. When you are both moving toward God and His values, you will be moving toward each other as well.

Love for your husband follows your love for God. You will spend all your earthly days together. Long after your children leave home, you will still be with your mate, Lord willing. The foundation you build with your husband flavors all other relationships in your life—your children, your extended family, and your friends.

Love for your children follows love for your husband. It would be easy to put the children first, because caring for children demands so much time. However, if you haven't firmly established a good relationship with your husband, you will struggle when the children are on their own. You will also struggle raising the children if your marriage is not solid. When you have a good marriage, the years after the children leave are a precious time for the two of you. Many child-development experts agree: the thing children crave most in the world are parents who love each other.

The dictionary definition of husband ("the master of a house; the male partner in marriage") hardly does justice to the personage of a husband. What is your definition of a husband?

Mentally describe your husband. How does he fit your definition?

Loving Your Husband Is a Choice

Love is always a choice of actions—not just an emotion. So when things get difficult, we must choose to love. We should not say, "I don't feel love for him anymore." When things get difficult, God asks us to love through our actions.

It is so good to know that the idea of loving your husband was created by God. It is His plan. Knowing that the Lord always wants your marriage to work is a great encouragement. If you are struggling with loving your husband, ask the Lord to help you. Ask Him to return to you the passion and love you felt at first.

Write out Psalm 37:4:

What relationship does the Lord desire from you? How does He respond to you?

If you have an ongoing special situation in your marriage, such as abusive behavior, or unfaithfulness, you need to seek professional help and guidance. In 1 Corinthians 7:4-5, the Lord does make provision for a season of being apart physically, by mutual consent, specifically for the purpose of prayer for healing.

Read Matthew 5:27-37 from Jesus' greatest sermon. Jesus deals with adultery, divorce, and the sacredness of oaths. How do these topics relate to each other?

Sometimes you or your spouse may seem "unlovable" because of a trial or situation in your marriage. Perhaps that is why Jesus described the tools for loving the unlovable right after He discussed the importance of fulfilling the marriage commitment.

How have you and your husband acted in "unlovable" ways? Think through some steps you could take to change those patterns. List some here:

1 Corinthians 13:4-8 gives us the proper concept of love. Memorize these verses, so that God can use them to encourage you.

"Love is patient, love is kind. It does not envy, it does not boast, it is not proud. It is not rude, it is not self-seeking, it is not easily angered, it keeps no record of wrongs. Love does not delight in evil but rejoices with the truth. It always protects, always trusts, always hopes, always perseveres. Love never fails."

Before we can understand, desire, and fulfill this kind of love in our marriage, we need to have a right relationship with the Lord. When Christ is our first love, He enhances our marriage by helping us understand one another. Your marriage is a testimony. Make sure it is a positive one. It is God's desire that your marriage is joyful. He will help you when you are obedient and when you ask for and desire His will.

One definition of love is "giving to someone's basic needs without having as my motive personal reward."

In working with clients for over twenty years, Dr. Willard F. Harley, Jr., has identified in his book *His Needs, Her Needs* the five most important needs for men and women as:

He found that by identifying and meeting each other's most important needs, your love and desire for each other will grow. Does it surprise you that the needs men expressed were different from the ones women expressed?

Plan a time to tell your husband what you need. Don't make him guess how you feel. Plan this for a time when you both are relaxed. Have a cup of tea and start talking. Calmly, but clearly, make your feelings known. Ask him how he thinks and feels about you. Discuss what changes need to be made for you to experience greater joy in your marriage. Issues can be resolved more quickly when you understand each other and when each of you knows what the other wants and expects from your marriage.

In this study we will concentrate on the five most common needs husbands express and ways to meet them.

Meeting His Need for Physical Love

Song of Solomon is sometimes viewed as being a picture of Christ's love for His people. More often, however, it is thought to be a collection of love poems between a lover and his beloved. It is also a picture of God's ideal for love and marriage.

Husbands
- sexual fulfillment
- recreational companionship
- an attractive spouse
- domestic support
- admiration

Wives
- affection
- conversation
- honesty and openness
- financial support
- family commitment

Write out Song of Solomon 8:7:

Take the time to read the Song of Solomon. Can you relate your marriage to passages in this book? Read a chapter each day this week of study.

Are you romantic? Do certain romantic songs and movies affect your mood? Make time to turn your romantic longings into actions. Though my friends Milan and Linda have been married over thirty-five years, there is still romance in their lives. They end each prayer with a kiss—no matter where they are (even in a restaurant or at a friend's house). "Their song" is "Moon River." One day they were riding in the car along a country road early in the morning. "Moon River" came on the radio. Linda said, "That makes me want to dance with you." Milan stopped the car along the road, turned the radio up, took Linda's hand, and danced with her along the road. I love that story. Expressing your romantic feelings is a marriage protector!

When you first see your husband after you've been apart, express your affection for him—no matter what kind of day you have had! The love you show will be appreciated and sets the mood for the evening. "Business" can wait until later.

It is also very important not to neglect sexual intimacy. The physical aspect of marriage is the number one need many men express. It is also important to God, and it must be important to us. The gift of sex is the gift that only you can give to your husband. You are the only one who can fulfill his need for physical intimacy.

Physical intimacy is basic to a sense of closeness and security. When things go wrong in a relationship, touching seems to stop first. If you need help with this part of your marriage, seek it.

Read 1 Corinthians 7:5. Withholding love from your mate is a sin. It is, however, one way some wives choose to "hurt" their husbands when they are angry. Even in the midst of arguments, physical love cannot be the issue.

Be more concerned about your husband's needs than about your own. Ask him what he needs. Be absolutely determined to show physical love to your husband. It is up to him to be concerned for your needs. Tell him what you need to be happy and satisfied.

Meeting His Need for Recreational Companionship

Write out Genesis 2:18:

When Adam was alone in the Garden of Eden, his work was caring for the garden—a pleasant recreation in the days before weeds! Yet God saw his need for companionship and created a helper for Adam. Husbands still desire the recreational companionship of their wives.

What common activities do you and your husband share?

Ask him to rank them by how much he enjoys them. Then ask your husband to choose one or two activities (on or off the list) he would like to spend more time doing with you. Plan a time to do them. If this will be a financial or time squeeze, be creative. Perhaps you can trade child care with other Apples of Gold participants or substitute a less costly activity you can both genuinely enjoy that doesn't center on the kids. The important thing is to explore options until you find activities that meet that special need.

Meeting His Need for an Attractive Spouse

Read Proverbs 31:22. Why do you think her garments and her bedspread were mentioned together in this verse? For whom was she dressing?

My friend Lori grew up with the Christian value that it is what's inside that counts. Physical appearance is just the frame around the real you—your character and personality! And she had lots of Scripture verses to back her up. So she felt comfortable going for a short, "easy" haircut. Then her husband, Scott, said, "You're the only wife I have, and I want to enjoy the way you look. Can I choose your hairstyle?"

So Scott interviewed Lori's hairstylist to figure out all the styles that would work for Lori. He picked having Lori grow her hair long. (Does this surprise you?)

As a gift of love, be neat and clean. Smell wonderful! Ask your husband which of your outfits (casual, dressy, and sleepwear) are his favorites.

What steps will you take to give your husband the gift of a spouse that is pleasing in his eyes?

Meeting His Need for Domestic Support

How do you think your home feels to your husband when he comes home at the end of the day?

Make your home a haven, so that being home with you outshines being away from home.

For some of us, this may mean a total overhaul. Pick up. Organize. And if the whole house can't be straightened up the way he likes it, make sure he has one clean room he can enjoy.

Because kids can mess up a house faster than you can clean it, talk with your husband about setting reasonable standards for your household. The important thing is to respect his need for order, even if you can't always meet it.

Cook wonderful meals for him. Plan variety into your meals. Plan ahead. Find out his favorites and make them. One wife asked her husband to write each of his favorite meals on index cards. She rotates them for meal planning. However, it is also exciting to try new menus from time to time. Perhaps he will find a new favorite!

When both spouses work a forty-hour week, a wife can resent the idea that another full-time job awaits her at home. Yet even in homes where both spouses share the domestic tasks, many men feel "loved" when their wives do certain chores that make a home for him. Even if your husband willingly vacuums, cooks, and does dishes, there may be something that will fill his love bank, whether it's eating a lunch you packed just for him, sitting down to your meatloaf once a week, or knowing you keep his favorite shirt clean because he really likes it. The important thing is to find out what those symbolic tasks are. The rest can be divided between you or hired out.

Meeting His Need for Admiration

Write out Proverbs 12:25:

Your opinion of your husband has great impact on him. He loves to live up to your expectations and thrives on your honest compliments. Be interested in his work and projects. Become the number one member of his fan club, and offer your kids free memberships.

Write out Philippians 4:8:

Looking at Paul's list here, what are we to emphasize?

State your wants and needs without complaining, nagging, and criticizing. A little sugar goes a long way. Keep a photograph of your husband as a child where you can see it often; it will help you remember how far he's come and how fragile his feelings can be. "A gentle answer turns away wrath" (Prov. 15:1).

Read Proverbs 12:4a and 31:23, 28. How does a loving wife benefit her husband?

Today the "city gate" would probably be your husband's place of employment, the church, and your neighborhood. The way you speak of your husband is often the way others know him. What can you do to be sure your husband is respected?

3) Keep from sharing family disagreements with others. Try never to "nurse" an insult you received. The tension will pass in a few days, but it is difficult to take back the words you should not have spoken.

Make sure that you build up your husband, privately and publicly. Don't make him look bad or embarrass him in front of others—ever!

Of course, there is sometimes a need to share family problems. If problems in your marriage are ongoing, talk with your pastor or a friend who you know is wise and completely trustworthy, and seek professional help when needed.

Choice Fruit
Honoring Your Vows

Read Proverbs 5 and 1 Corinthians 7:10, 39. Jot down ideas that speak to your heart about faithfulness to your husband.

Faithfulness should be a given in a Christian marriage. But today, unfaithfulness, even in Christian marriages, is a problem, and divorce is affecting the church in a serious way. People involved in the sin of unfaithfulness, as well as their families, pay a heavy price.

Read Proverbs 31:10-11. Does your husband fully trust you? Are you fully worthy of his trust?

God expects you to be 100 percent faithful to your mate as long as you live. Ask the Lord to keep you from the temptation to "look," to "flirt," and to otherwise tempt your senses.

Write out Hebrews 13:4:

Loving your husband and protecting your marriage is not always an easy job. You need the Lord's help to keep you on track and to correct problems. He wants you to succeed, so remember to ask His help every day.

Obedience to God Brings Blessings

Read Proverbs 5:18-19. Being married to you should be a cause for rejoicing!

How does the love you show for your husband benefit:

• your family?

• your friends and church family?

Keep the flame of love burning. Remember often the wonderful times you have shared, forgive quickly, and forget the difficult times. Don't go to bed angry. Keep dating, and have fun together!

Prayer

Author of love, thank You for the mate You have given to me. He is precious to me, and I want our marriage to be pleasing to You. Help me, Father, to delight in my husband, to desire to please him, and to give him my love and affection freely.

Keep me from the sins of the world: the staggering amount of sexual sin that is around me. Give me a deep desire to be pure in my relationship to You and to my husband.

And give me words of love daily, Lord. Help me speak the language of love to my husband, so that his desire will always be for me alone.

Thank You, Lord, that You created marriage, and that You want to help me to live for You. I ask this in Your precious name. Amen.

For Further Reading

Willard F. Harley, Jr., *His Needs, Her Needs: Building an Affair-Proof Marriage* (Grand Rapids, Mich.: Fleming Revell, 1994). (The categories in this lesson are based on Dr. Harley's helpful book.)

Jerry B. Jenkins, *Loving Your Marriage Enough to Protect It* (Chicago: Moody Press, 1993).

Elisabeth Elliot, *Let Me Be a Woman* (Wheaton, Ill.: Tyndale House Publishers, 1976).

Jill Briscoe and her daughter Judy Golz, *Space to Breathe, Room to Grow* (Nashville, Tenn.: Oliver-Nelson Books, 1985).

Dan Seaborn, *One-Minute Devotionals for Couples* (Indianapolis, Ind.: Wesleyan Publishing House, 1996).

 Suggestions for the Leader

1 If time permits, have a few women share their Apple Seeds. Be prepared to share a bit of your own love story.

2 In your discussion, try to bring out that a right relationship with the Lord will lead to a sense of forgiveness (which helps us admit our mistakes); humility (because we will know God and others have played such a big role in our success); a healthy self-esteem (because we know God has chosen us and has a purpose for our lives); obedience to God and His laws; putting others before self; and the fruit of the Spirit: love, joy, peace, patience, self-control.

3 Show the women a tube of toothpaste. As you squeeze the tube onto a plate, say: "These are my negative comments to others about my husband. Even as you could try all day and never get all the toothpaste back into the tube, once you've said those words, they can never be unsaid. It's so important to watch your words."

*". . . Train the young women to love their husbands and children, to be
sensible, chaste, domestic, kind, and submissive to their husbands, that the
word of God may not be discredited." Titus 2:3–5 (RSV)*

Lesson Three

Loving Your Children

A Mother's Prayer

*I pray for you, my child, a life that's filled with laughter;
That you will know the joy of Christ within your soul.
And when temptations come, I pray that you will trust Him,
Knowing He holds all things in His control.
I pray for you, my child, that you will know the Father,
And trust in Jesus Christ, His one and only Son,
And may the Holy Spirit's favor rest upon you
Until your race for Him on earth is done.*
—B.H.

Apple Seeds

Set the mood by singing "A Mother's Prayer" (music on p. 141).

1. Take a look at a favorite photograph of each of your children. What do you love most about each child?

Apple Blossoms

Loving your child does not only involve the natural feelings of your heart; it involves teaching, caring, nurturing, and discipline. Sometimes it seems natural and easy; some days are just plain hard work.

The Word of God is our final authority. Let's look at some of the things God says in His Word about caring for your children.

Dedicate Your Children to God

 Read Psalm 127. What does it mean for the Lord to build your house?

What blessings and results can you expect if the Lord is building your house?

Blessings   **Results**

If the Lord is building your house, you can be greatly encouraged. His promises are great to you. If you have not yet made the decision to dedicate your home and children to the Lord, and have Him truly be the Head, you will struggle in your efforts to raise your children. The Bible is a handbook for parents. Take advantage of the Lord's advice and promises.

Reread Psalm 127:3. What does it mean to you that your children are a heritage from the Lord?

Throughout Scripture, the Lord talks about heritage, your children's children, your extended family. Read Exodus 20:5-6, Deuteronomy 4:9, Psalm 22:30-31, and Proverbs 17:6.

What you do with and for your children has results and/or consequences far beyond your lifetime. Think about that! How do you want to be remembered as a parent and grandparent to future generations?

How do you remember your parents and grandparents?

It is a blessing that you have the opportunity to follow the positive examples of your parents and grandparents or correct mistakes that were made. We can follow the instructions of our Creator. The key is to be teachable ourselves.

Take Comfort in God's Love for Your Child

You can trust your children to the Lord's care. As much as you love your children, God loves them so much more.

Jot down an example of a time you felt God's love was demonstrated to you and your family.

List a few key attributes of your child. How has your knowledge of that child helped you protect and care for him or her? (For example, easing a shy child into a new situation.)

The Lord knew your children from your womb (Jer. 1:5). He knows all their needs. Try to rest in the comfort that He understands your child's needs when you don't seem to know how to handle a situation.

Remember that you are also God's child. He cares for you and wants to protect you in the same way that you care for and protect your children.

Be Sensitive

Read Romans 12:15. Part of valuing our children is valuing their emotions. Let them share their emotions with you. By listening, you will show them you really care, and don't think they are silly when they think or feel something deeply. If you allow them to express their sadness, they will be more willing to work through their sad feelings and move on.

Can you remember a time when your child was deeply hurt? How did you respond?

How did your child respond to you? What told your child that you really cared?

Experience Joy

Teach joy to your children. The old saying is still true, "JOY stands for Jesus, Others, then Yourself." Let them know that joy comes from obedience to God and to their parents.

Write out Proverbs 15:30:

Look for fun and happiness in everyday happenings. Learn to laugh! Don't be afraid to be laughed at when you do something that seems funny to your children. Laugh at yourself. It teaches your children it is okay to laugh at themselves. Perhaps you can tell about something silly you did as a child. Laugh about it with them. They will then feel safe to tell you about some silly things they have done.

My "grands" love to hear stories about their parents when they were young. They coax my husband, Lee, and me to tell "just one more"; then they go home and tell their parents. It is great fun!

Write out Proverbs 17:22:

Write out Psalm 15:13:

Is your child's heart more cheerful because of the expression on your face? What kind of "looks" do you give your children? How do you want them to remember your face? Remember that children are good "face readers" and that if your spirit is "crushed," your child will see that as well.

Your relationship with the Lord greatly affects the mood in the home. If you struggle with joy in your own life, it will be difficult to pass joy on to your children. What is the mood in your home?

What can you do to create a more positive mood in your home?

When you see your child experiencing joy, ask, "What did you like about this activity?" This has been called the Golden Question because it can unlock the mystery of your child's motivated abilities. You may be surprised by the answer. You might think your triumphant little artist liked drawing the picture (and you were ready to sign her up for art lessons) only to hear, "I knew it would make you smile, Mom!" Her real motivated ability was serving others, not necessarily art. (For a full explanation of the Golden Question, see Ralph Mattson and Thom Black's book, *Discovering Your Child's Design*, listed in For Further Reading.)

Write out Psalm 119:111:

Knowing and obeying the Word brings joy to our hearts. We need to be in the Word of God daily in order to have a positive and joyful attitude.

Teach the Word of God to Your Children

Write out Deuteronomy 11:18-21:

Do you realize that this means you are to teach your children all the time? What a great challenge!

These verses are commands of the Lord, and we need to take them seriously. They are not suggestions. If we desire to be obedient to God, we will enjoy teaching His precepts to our children.

What keeps you from accomplishing this?

What steps can you take this week to make teaching the Word of God a regular part of your family's routine?

Discipline: Determining the Essentials

Teaching your children to obey both you and God is a big part of raising them. The ultimate goal is for them to develop the inner discipline that allows them to do what is right when no one is watching, to do the will of God from their hearts (Eph. 6:6).

Discipline is an important part of a child's development, and it is essential for the results you are seeking. An undisciplined child does not know boundaries. We all need boundaries, and we need to understand what they are. Some examples of boundaries may be bedtimes, coming the first time called, talking respectfully, and so on. Undisciplined children bring sorrow to their parents.

Write out Proverbs 22:15:

Write out Proverbs 23:13-14:

How do you understand these verses?

What do these verses mean to you?

Concentrate on five "forever qualities" that you think are important for your children. These are five rules that must be kept, five goals to strive for. Focus on these five qualities even if you have to let go of some other goals. Too many negative rules can produce rebellion. Be sure you stress the positive side of the goals you make.

Forever qualities might include:
· Demonstrating love, respect, and obedience to God
· Demonstrating love, respect, and obedience to parents
· Demonstrating love and respect for siblings and extended family
· Being trustworthy
· Being responsible about schoolwork
· Being a good friend
· Acting responsibly
· Showing kindness, gentleness, and patience

What are the essentials for your family? Determine this with your spouse.
1.
2.
3.
4.
5.

Write these goals somewhere special to remind yourselves.

Write out brief, clear descriptions (less than 250 words) so that your children know what is expected of them. Explain why you think these things are important issues and how these qualities will aid them throughout their lives.

Talk through any questions and objections they may have.

Once the goals are established, review them daily, at first, so that your children are constantly aware of the goals.

Then catch your children at being good! Remember how excited you were when your toddler made the smallest progress at walking? You would drop everything to applaud. Be that enthusiastic again. Children thrive on your loving encouragement. As they experience the rewards of meeting their goals, they will develop the inner motivation needed to exchange old habits for new. Let your children know that you will be watching for progress.

It is important that you know there will be setbacks. Pray with your children every day to encourage them along the way. Listen intently when they tell you they don't agree. Try to brainstorm together solutions that fit a situation. Children can be very creative! Let them know that their opinion matters to you, but also that sometimes they just need to do as you say.

Read Proverbs 3:12. According to this verse, a reprimand should communicate two things: discipline and love. No matter what happens, your children need to know that they are loved.

Before you begin to discipline, think of how you want the situation to end. The following process offers both discipline and love.

1. Get your child's attention.

2. State clearly the rule or goal that was disregarded.

3. Explain how this makes you feel.

4. Explain why this behavior is unacceptable. Focus on the behavior without tearing down the child's personality.

5. Pause to let this sink in.

6. In a calm tone of voice, tell your child how much you love and value him or her. Give your child a hug of reassurance.

7. Express your confidence that your child can and will do better.

(For a fuller explanation of this process, see *The One-Minute Mother* by Dr. Spencer Johnson, listed in For Further Reading.)

Think of a recent confrontation with your child. Use the steps above to resolve it.

Discipline Issue:

1.

2.

3.

4.

5.

6.

7.

If you are too angry to express your love and confidence, it's a signal you are too angry to discipline effectively. If you discipline a child while you are angry, you may regret it. It may cause you to say or do something you would never say or do otherwise. Take some time to cool off, but be sure to deal with the issue. It often seems easier not to discipline or to wait until you have a big problem. There are consequences for neglecting discipline. Bad habits will be firmly entrenched, and your child will learn to manipulate you.

The time invested in your child's life will bear fruit. Proverbs 31 describes a wise woman. In verse 28 it says "her children arise and call her blessed." I believe they blessed her because she coupled discipline with love.

Prayer

Heavenly Father, thank You for the gift of children. Thank You for the privilege of being a mother.

I acknowledge my need for Your wisdom and guidance day by day. Thank You for Your Word and the joy and guidance it brings to my life.

Teach me to enjoy the personalities and talents of the children You have created for me to enjoy. Help us to laugh often, to sing and read and pray together, so that these precious children feel secure and loved.

Lord Jesus, help me to be a good daughter to my parents and to enjoy them! Help me to say "I love you" often.

Help me to find time to be refreshed in my busy schedule, to be sure my mate does not feel left out, and to make sure he feels my love. Most of all, Heavenly Father, help me to make time for You every day, for without You, I will surely fail. Amen.

Helpful Parenting Tips

Make Your Child Feel Special!

Make memorable times with your children—even on ordinary days. Keep a Special Occasion Diary with your children. This helps them to see a pattern of special things you do together and creates a positive memory bank from which they can draw throughout their lives. Make holiday traditions that are yours alone. Make birthdays into occasions to remember.

Make time to be alone with each child. What are your child's interests? Find activities to bring out that interest in your child. Later on you can help them to be more interested in your interests as well. Find a way to show them how exciting it can be to learn new things. For example, teach your daughter how to cook!

If your child has special interests that you know little about, take the time to learn about them or find a friend who can help you. Perhaps you have a gift that you can share with your friend's child. Don't be threatened by the involvement of other good people in your child's life. Encourage your child to reach out to other trustworthy adults. It will help them with their social development.

Teach Good Manners to Your Children

When children are taught good manners at an early age, manners become a natural part of their life. When your children are taught good table manners, it is not uncomfortable for them (or you) to go to a nice restaurant for dinner. It's fun to turn your dining room into Chez Mom Café (complete with the good dinnerware and menus) to give young ones the experience of "fine dining." Other times you can arrange leftovers in a buffet line so children learn how to fill their plates with enough but not too much. With some practice, they will know what to do, and you will not be correcting them in a restaurant. You will save yourself and your child embarrassment. (For more on this, see Chapter 11 of Barbara Coloroso's book, *Kids Are Worth It!*)

Another wonderful book about manners for children is *The Family Book of Manners*, written by a good friend, Hermine Hartley. (See for further reading) Some things included in Hermine's book are:

- How to meet and greet people
- How to behave in church or an auditorium
- Proper table etiquette
- How to be a good guest in a friend's home

If you are unsure about proper etiquette yourself, there are excellent books available. Consider one a worthwhile investment. Any complete book of etiquette will be helpful, such as Letitia Baldrige's edition of *The Amy Vanderbilt Complete Book of Etiquette* (New York: Doubleday, 1978).

Memorize Scripture Together

One of life's greatest treasures is knowing the Word, and your children will never forget the verses they learn now. It is amazing how often verses we learned as children come to us in a difficult time, or in happy times, to remind us of the faithfulness of God.

Start early, and praise success! Start with easier or partial verses for little ones, and have the older children learn the entire verse.

Set up a Memory Verse File System (one for each family member). Here's how:

Get a three-by-five card file. With taller cards, separate the box into three categories: Verses I Am Learning, Verses I Have Learned, and Verses I Want to Learn. When you begin to study a verse, write it on an index card and file it in the first category. When it is memorized, move it to the "Have Learned" section in book order (Genesis before Exodus, etc.). Continually review the "Have Learned" verses by positioning a tall marker card behind the last verse you've said by heart. (This will remind you to review verses, not just "memorize" them and then forget them.)

A great verse to start with is Psalm 119:11: "I have hidden your word in my heart that I might not sin against you."

Have Daily Devotions with Your Children

Proverbs 20:11 says, "Even a child is known by his actions, by whether his conduct is pure and right." Knowing the Word develops your child's attitude and personality.

In teaching your children, be creative and be consistent. Know what time works for your family, and then follow through. For some, dinnertime is best; for others, bedtime. Perhaps after school is a good time to snuggle and have a story. Just do it! And be sure to encourage your children to express their feelings and ideas about the story.

Read a short Bible passage, or have your children read. Pray together and sing a song. Make it a habit; it will become a tradition! It is wonderful to see the next generation following through with the same traditions. I remember sitting on my father's lap after dinner while he read the Bible. Sometimes when I came home from college, I would still sit on his lap during family devotions. It's a special memory.

Teach Your Children How to Sing

Learn hymns and choruses. They will always be a great encouragement! Encourage your children to accompany you on rhythm instruments until they are ready for something more.

There are numerous Scriptures about singing to the Lord. What is your favorite? Make it your inspiration!

Encouragement for Mom

This may not seem to fit in a lesson about children, but if a mom is struggling in her life, it will be very difficult for her to encourage her children.

Motherhood is wonderful! It can also be trying and lonely at times. Some moms

have shared that they feel lonely or isolated even with children in the house. Other moms may never understand or feel that loneliness.

If you are a person who sometimes feels lonely, know that God is always with you and cares about your loneliness. Seek Him for guidance, and cast all your cares on Him.

Develop some good friendships. Friendships don't just happen. Sometimes you need to take the initiative. Developing good friendships takes time, but the effort is worthwhile. Ask the Lord to lead you to friends who will be good for you and with whom you can share. He cares about such things. He created us to desire fellowship with others. Though we need to be friendly to everyone, we do not need to be close friends with everyone. There is a difference! We are all different in our needs and interests.

A mature Christian friend is a treasure! Pray that you will find a wise Christian friend. Find a mentor who is trustworthy. Accept her wisdom as a gift from God to you.

Look for some friends who are fun-loving and who share similar interests. Don't expect them to find you—you find them!

Don't think in terms of what you will get in a relationship but rather what you can offer. Serve in a personal, Christlike manner.

Look for friends who are good for you, as well as those who may need you. Perhaps you have children the same age; maybe you are not even close in age. Sometimes a friend who is older or younger will be more stimulating to you.

Finding another family with interests similar to yours is another good idea and fun for all. Remember, having fun is important!

Be sure to have more than one friend because friends can move away, or become busy with something or someone else.

Find someone who can give you a break once in a while. Then return the favor to her. You and your friend will both be refreshed.

For Further Reading

J. Otis and Gail Ledbetter, *Heritage Builders: Family Fragrance* (Colorado Springs, Colo.: Chariot Victor Publishing, 1998).

Ralph Mattson and Thom Black, *Discovering Your Child's Design* (Elgin, Ill.: David C. Cook Publishing Co., 1989).

Stuart and Jill Briscoe, *The Family Book of Christian Values* (Colorado Springs, Colo.: Alive Communications, Inc., 1995).

Carol Ardizzone, *Motherhood, The Proverbs 31 Ministry* (call 1-877-P31-HOME).

Evelyn Christenson, *What Happens When We Pray for Our Families* (Colorado Springs, Colo.: Chariot Victor Publishing, 1992).

Hermine Hartley, *The Family Book of Manners* (Uhrichsville, Ohio: Barbour and Company, Inc.).

Spencer Johnson, *The One Minute Mother* (New York: William Morrow, 1983).

Adele Faber and Elaine Mazlish, *How to Talk So Kids Will Listen & Listen So Kids Will Talk* (New York: Avon, 1982).

Barbara Coloroso, *Kids Are Worth It! Giving Your Child the Gift of Inner Discipline* (New York: William Morrow, 1994).

D. Ross Campbell, *How to Really Love Your Child* (Colorado Springs, Colo.: Chariot Victor Publishing, 1980).

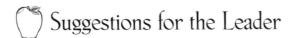 Suggestions for the Leader

 If time permits, have a few participants share their Apple Seeds.

 Share an example of how the Lord is building your own house.

Get a few packets of flower seeds. Sprinkle a few of the same type of seed into an envelope. Make enough envelopes for each woman present. Label the envelopes with a number or a letter so you know which flower it corresponds to, but don't identify the seed by name on the envelope. (If you cannot find seeds, use herb seeds from your kitchen. A gardening book will tell you how they grow.)

Pass out the envelopes, with a photocopy of the following questions:

You've been given an unknown seed.
• When can it be planted outside?
• What kind of soil does it need?
• How deep should it be planted?
• How much space does it need?
• How much water does it need?
• How soon will it begin to grow?
• Will it thrive in sun or shade?

(If time permits, you might want to share the answers to the A seed, etc., but this is not important to the point of the illustration.)

Ask: "Who here experienced a sense of bewilderment when you were handed the seed packet—a feeling of 'How should I know?' Have you ever felt that way handling your child?

"In a very real sense, each of your children is like an unknown seed that God has entrusted to your care. You may find yourself saying, 'How do I help this child?' God wants to hear that question from you—often! And He wants you to be open to the answer. Only God knows the unique needs and attributes of that special person who is your child. God knew your child fully even in your womb (Jer. 1:5). That is why you need to stay close to God in prayer, asking Him to guide you to the right words, gestures, opportunities, and teachers for your child. This will take humility and submission on your part, because your child may be very different from you. Faith is 'seeing what God intends to do in a situation and acting in harmony with it.' As a God-honoring parent, you need to have faith in the unique plan God has for this seed, your precious child."

 Having family devotions can seem like a daunting undertaking. If time permits, share a story of a successful series of devotions you had with your family. Or have another participant share. Stress that willingness to find the time and learn together is the chief prerequisite! Have some family devotional books handy to show the women.

". . . Train the young women to love their husbands and children, to be sensible, chaste, domestic, kind, and submissive to their husbands, that the word of God may not be discredited." Titus 2:3–5 (RSV)

Lesson Four

Submission

I submit, O Father, to Your will and way.
And I treasure every word that you say.
Help me to understand Your wisdom and Your plan.
And keep me knitted in the palm of Your hand.
—B.H.

Apple Seeds

Set the mood by singing "I Submit, O Father" (music on p. 142).

1 What is your idea of submission? How did the words of the song above cast a new light on the idea of submission for you?

Apple Blossoms

Submitting to Others Begins with Submitting to God

The idea of submission is not always a popular one. We have our own ideas of what submission means. Sometimes we think it means giving up our own ideas or giving up something that is important to us.

Yet the same God who says, "Submit to one another out of reverence for Christ" (Eph. 5:21) also assures us: "'. . . I know the plans I have for you,' declares the LORD, 'plans to prosper you and not to harm you, plans to give you hope and a future'" (Jer. 29:11).

Only learning more about what your loving God wants and expects to accomplish through your submission will help you reconcile this seeming contradiction!

Read Matthew 8:5-13. Jesus was astonished by the centurion's understanding of His role in the world. What was Jesus' evaluation of this man?

Jesus was making a powerful statement. The centurion realized that just as his life was based on a chain of responsibility, the kingdom of God is set up in much the same way. Faith has been defined as "seeing what God intends to do in a situation and acting in harmony with it." How did the centurion demonstrate such faith?

The centurion was a man who stood under authority and saw God work on his behalf. Standing under God's authority empowers us.

Webster's Dictionary pinpoints three aspects of submission:

1. To yield (oneself) to the authority or control of another; to surrender.
2. To subject a person or thing to a process.
3. To be willing to obey.

These definitions point out many ways we, as Christians, submit to God. Submission is a daily happening. It's something that comes up over and over during the day. Describe a time you experienced each kind of submission. How did the certainty that God had your best in mind make submitting easier?

• Yielding to God's authority:

• Making yourself available to God's process of correction or growth in your life:

• Being willing to obey when disobeying seemed more practical:

Do you sometimes find it difficult to submit to the authority of God? Cite an example. Why do you find this true for yourself?

You must learn to believe that God is absolutely trustworthy, that He only wants what is best for you, and that His love for you is perfect. What a comfort to know that even submission is given by the Lord because He truly desires what is best for you. He has established His guidelines because He loves you so much!

Submitting to Others
Out of Reverence for Christ

It is easier to submit to a perfect God than to an imperfect person. Yet, when God establishes the boundaries of submission, you can trust Him, because He is perfect.

Write out Ephesians 5:21:

Many people have the misconception that submission is an issue for women alone. However, the Word of God says that we are to submit to one another.

Why would this be done "out of reverence for Christ"?

God designed submission to bless your life! It is the very essence of the Christian life. When you submit to the will of God and obey the Word of God, you have discovered the way of blessing. There are consequences to choosing a path of not submitting to the will and Word of God.

Read Luke 2:49-52. What did Jesus' obedience to His parents bring?

Read 1 Samuel 15:23. Disobedience to God opens your life up to Satan's authority. What is rebellion compared to in this passage?

Submission is not about your worth or value, but it is important for a balanced life. In the world, authority rules others. In the Christian world, leadership serves others. Read Philippians 2:1-11. How do these verses explain this teaching?

Read Titus 2:9-10. What was Paul's goal for submission here?

(2) Learning to submit to a higher authority begins when we are children. Children who are taught the godly way of submission to those in authority over them will find it easier to submit later in life. They will learn not to feel threatened by someone with authority over them.

It can be a great relief to submit to someone you trust. Sometimes we do not have an answer to a dilemma in our life and we need to trust the decisions to others. Children should be able to trust the decisions of their parents. For Christian families, the children need to know that their parents are submitting to the Lord first of all.

Write out Hebrews 13:7:

Write out Romans 13:1:

What assurance does God give us that we can submit to leaders in our schools, community, and country even if they are not Christians?

Read Daniel 1:3-17. Part of submission is learning to offer a respectful appeal. Daniel "resolved not to defile himself" (verse 8) with the king's unclean food. He displayed a mature attitude in dealing with the chief official. His respectful attitude and creative suggestion gained him "loving favor"—and his request.

How did he affirm the guard's authority? Note what he said and how he said it.

Daniel approached the official with a cooperative, loving spirit. He had a clear conscience, knowing he had not resisted the official in the past. Daniel discerned the basic intention of the official's request (to make the men healthy and strong). Then he offered a creative alternative that met that same goal. Daniel suggested the chief official test his suggestion. Daniel trusted that God would strengthen him and his friends on the simple diet of vegetables and water. The improvement was so great, the chief official was won over.

Read James 3:13-18. Write out verses 17-18:

By following the example in James 3:13-18, how can you apply this to submission in your life?

The James passage is soft and sweet, isn't it? It helps us put it all together in a way that makes sense and brings peace to our lives.

Read Proverbs 15:22. Bearing in mind what you've learned about submission, how would you submit to . . .

• Your parents, now that you are an adult:

· Your supervisor (whether you are paid or a volunteer):

· Your child:

· Your friend:

· Your government:

Choice Fruit

Submission in Marriage

Submission to our husbands begins with submission to God. If we are not willing to submit to the authority of God and Scripture, it is not likely that we will submit to our husbands.

When couples understand the true meaning of submission as outlined in the Bible, they can think of submission as an active, joyful participation instead of just a passive obedience.

Write out 1 Corinthians 11:8-9, 11-12:

God did create us, male and female, with a will. He also created some of us with stronger wills than others. Some of us see any advice or admonition of another to be an invasion of our wills, and we have a quick wall that goes up. We say, "Don't tell me what is right and wrong." Other people are passive and never express their feelings and desires. Neither of those responses is helpful in a relationship. Learning to properly communicate our feelings in love is the way to grow together. It is a process.

Learning to accept sound advice helps us grow. When we submit to God's way and yield to one another, and when each wants what is truly best for the other, submission becomes easy and rewarding.

Write out 1 Corinthians 11:3:

The Greek word for head means "source," like the source of a river.

God the Father is the source of all life and relationships. Everything proceeds from Him. He has established an order of submission in our relationships. There is a progression of showing honor or respect.

Some scholars see the term head as primarily a concept of honor, as one's physical head represents his or her honor. So as Christ honored God, a man should honor Christ, and a woman should honor her husband. Others read the word head as a symbol of authority, which would also encompass the concept of honor, because Paul uses the term to mean "authority" in Ephesians 1:21-22 ("under his feet," "head over everything"). In other words, as Christ is in authority over a man and is due honor by him, so a husband is in a position of authority and should be honored by his wife.

 Sometimes a decision must be made on an important issue, and there is a disagreement between you and your husband. Perhaps you have made some creative appeals, but your husband has not agreed to them. You need to pray that your husband will submit to and know the will of God in this matter. God's will for you is to support him in the decision he makes.

Has this happened in your marriage? Give an example.

How did God honor your obedience?

Write out Ephesians 5:21-24:

Write out Ephesians 5:33:

 4 One of the most important needs of a husband is to be respected. It gives him confidence and honors his work and his relationships with others.

Write out Colossians 3:18-19:

These verses show the balance in submission that God requires. Just as the Lord deals lovingly with us, we are to deal lovingly with others. When your husband deals lovingly with you, it is much easier to respond in the same manner. And when you deal lovingly with him, he can respond in like manner to you.

"The same goes for you wives: Be good wives to your husbands, responsive to their needs. There are husbands who, indifferent as they are to any words about God, will be captivated by your life of holy beauty. What matters is not your outer appearance—the styling of your hair, the jewelry you wear, the cut of your clothes— but your inner disposition" (1 Peter 3:1-4, TM).

These verses are good advice to you if your husband is not a Christian. A husband who is not a believer is watching to see how you respond to and react to God and to him. And if your husband is a Christian, seeing you follow these verses will encourage him all the more to strive in his own Christian life.

In what ways will understanding this lesson help you to submit to others? Is there someone to whom you should submit and to whom you have refused to submit? How can the Word of God (and His promises) help you change?

Prayer

Dear Lord, submission is a difficult topic. You created me with a will and a sound mind. I am grateful for that. Yet my thoughts and desires are sometimes selfish, and I can be stubborn at times. I acknowledge that I need help from You.

Father in heaven, teach me to be willing to submit to You and to the precepts of Your Word. I know that You established order in my life and home for a good reason, and Your order brings peace and harmony.

I pray, Lord, for those in authority over me on this earth. I pray for the president, the local government, my pastors and church leaders, my parents and husband. Help me to pray for them faithfully. I ask that they will have Your wisdom and desire Your will, so that the decisions they make for me to follow are Yours.

I trust You today, Lord, to give me a clearer understanding of Your Word as it applies to submission. Have Your own way in my life today. Make me teachable. I love You, Lord. Amen.

Suggestions for the Leader

1 If time permits, have a few participants share their Apple Seeds.

2 Explain that part of submission is giving up the need to always be right. When it comes to parenting children, it becomes important to admit when you've been wrong or inconsistent and to ask forgiveness when you've made a mistake. Though children first learn to submit to our authority so they can learn to submit to God's, we can never confuse for them the fact that God is perfect and we are not.

One definition of submission was "to subject a person or thing to a process." In child rearing, God wants us to submit to the long, repetitive process of teaching our children, who are often slow to learn. If we accept the fact that it will take a long time, God will use the process to build new character qualities into our lives, as we try to help our children.

Often we, too, are slow to learn, and God is patient and persistent with us, drawing us closer to Him as we learn. This is also what happens when children learn: they are drawn closer to us.

 Describe a time you decided not to resist your husband's authority and the result was a far-reaching blessing.

 If time permits, point out how this ties in with the first two lessons. In the Kindness lesson we saw how destructive it is to talk about others behind their backs. In the Loving Your Husband lesson, we saw how much men desire affirmation.

A Penny for Your Thoughts

Many wives deeply desire their husbands to share their thoughts and feelings, and to lead the family. Sometimes it means examining your past responses to him, and making a few changes.

"Search me, O God, and know my heart;
test me and know my anxious thoughts.
See if there is any offensive way in me,
and lead me in the way everlasting."
Psalm 139:23-24

Is there room for improvement in the following ways?

• Give him a chance to talk about whatever is on his mind . . . and listen without interrupting.

• Allow times of companionable silence (even if it's tempting to fill up the space with talk).

• Make brief, encouraging responses that include restating what he's said, to show you want to understand.

• Offer advice only when it's asked for.

• Keep the talk positive, interesting, and fun.

• Welcome his constructive criticism—your defensiveness will quickly end the conversation.

• Apologize for times you have ignored his wishes and advice.

• Pray before you have a serious talk. It keeps the words sweeter.

"... Train the young women to love their husbands and children, to be sensible, chaste, domestic, kind, and submissive to their husbands, that the word of God may not be discredited." Titus 2:3–5 (RSV)

Lesson Five

Purity

Blest the pure in heart,
They shall see Your face.
As they gaze upon You,
Captured by Your grace.
Father, You alone
Are the Holy One.
Stamp upon my heart, Lord
The image of Your Son.
—B. H.

Apple Seeds

Set the mood by singing "Blest the Pure in Heart" (music on p. 142).

 Pick up the nearest secular magazine. As you glance, page by page, at the articles and photographs, use check marks to make a quick tally on the chart below:

Name of Periodical:

The High Road
(Number of items encouraging
noble thoughts and actions)

The Low Road
(Number of items encouraging poor
moral choices)

According to the results of your tally, what value does our society place on purity?

If convenient, bring the magazine to Apples of Gold class.

Apple Blossoms

Doing the right thing, rather than the thing that feels good, is a concept foreign to many people in our society today. Purity has always been an issue (the Bible has a lot to say about it), but our world is crumbling morally. We are made to think, by the media, books, and leaders, that morals change and even that they should change.

A dictionary would define purity this way: cleanness, freedom from physical or moral pollution, pureness, the state of being chaste.

A spiritual definition of purity would be: The moral excellence I demonstrate in my life as I consistently do what is right.

Purity involves thoughts, words, and actions. In this study, we will highlight purity in marriage—sexual purity. But we cannot have purity in marriage without purity of heart, mind, and spirit. Our entire nature is involved. It is a heart issue.

Think about your heart. Is it a dirty room where no light can enter? Or is it a clean room, where everything sparkles and the light reflects everywhere? God cannot use a dirty heart for His glory. God says, "Guard your heart, for it is the wellspring of life" (Prov. 4:23).

If you desire a pure heart, there is only one Person who can give it to you!

Read Psalm 51.
To whom is the psalmist speaking?

What does the psalmist ask God for in order to have a cleansed heart?
v. 2
v. 7
v. 10
v. 12

What are the results of having a cleansed heart?
v. 12
v. 13
v. 14-15

2 Asking for a cleansed heart is the single most important thing you can ever do. If you are unsure how to ask God for His forgiveness and need to understand how Christ paid for your sins on the cross, talk with an Apples of Gold mentor, your pastor, or a mature Christian friend.

Choice Fruit

Once you have a cleansed heart, keeping a pure heart becomes a day-by-day experience.

Read Proverbs 4:20-27. These verses give very good directions for guarding your heart. We will examine each aspect separately in our study of purity.

1. "Put away perversity from your mouth; keep corrupt talk far from your lips." (v. 24)
2. "Let your eyes look straight ahead, fix your gaze directly before you." (v. 25)
3. "Make level paths for your feet and take only ways that are firm." (v. 26)
4. "Do not swerve to the right or the left; keep your foot from evil." (v. 27)

1. Put Away Perversity from Your Mouth

In guarding your heart from impurity, a good place to start is with your thoughts, words, and attitudes. As we saw in our Kindness study, what goes down in the well, comes up in the bucket. If you want to keep corrupt talk far from your lips, you must cleanse your mind and heart. There are so many impure words, thoughts, movies, books, and ideas surrounding us today. They are so familiar that they can lose their shock value and seem harmless. But they aren't! Your mind is like a computer. It saves what goes in and makes it part of the master file. You need to be sure that what enters your mind is worth saving. What you think, you become. Purity of thought is essential for purity of action.

Write out Philippians 4:8:

Living in a society like ours, how can you follow this verse?

God establishes purity in your heart. You cannot attain it without His help.

A pure heart is not an automatic condition. It is created in you by the Lord through prayer, confession of sin, and a strong desire to be obedient.

If in the past you exposed your mind to impure influences, decide you will "flush out the bad" with heavy doses of Scripture and Christian teaching. Establishing the Word of God in your mind helps to keep your mind pure. Memorize meaningful verses and "psalms, hymns and spiritual songs" (Eph. 5:19-20). With God's help and conscious effort, you can rechannel your thought patterns.

Write out Psalm 19:14:

This is a good verse to memorize as a start-the-day prayer.

Read Matthew 12:34b. Purity of attitude results in purity of word. Are you careful about the words that you speak? Are your words a blessing to others? Are your words true? Are they trustworthy? Are your words sweet to the ear? Loving words are a decision. Make the decision to speak the truth in love!

Purity means you won't demean a friend, you won't gossip or say hurtful things about others. It means that you will choose to encourage rather than break down.

You need to nip a "bad day attitude" in the bud immediately and determine that with the help of God you will guard your heart. If you give Satan a toehold, he has your thoughts; if you give him a foothold, he has your attitudes; if you give him a stronghold, he has your way of life.

2. Fix Your Eyes Directly Before You

There is plenty to tempt you off the right path today and plenty of anti-Christian messages being proclaimed as truth. How do you cope? As the classic hymn by Helen Lemmel says,

> Turn your eyes upon Jesus,
> Look full in His wonderful face
> And the things of earth will grow strangely dim
> In the light of His glory and grace.

If you are tempted, the answer is to turn your eyes toward Jesus. Make Jesus your model of love and integrity, even when persecuted. His unchanging love for you can support you when you feel too weak to keep trying.

Read Proverbs 3:5-6. What does it mean to "acknowledge him"?

When you consider what Jesus would want of you in "all your ways," the result is "your path will be made straight"!

3. Take Only Ways That Are Firm

To "take only ways that are firm" means to make long-range choices and set boundaries for yourself. God commands this over and over!

Write out Isaiah 30:21:

The King James version of 1 Thessalonians 5:22 says to "abstain from all appearance of evil." If there is any way that something you do can be misinterpreted as evil or hurts your testimony and your heart, you must avoid it.

Write out Psalm 119:9-11:

The Word of God is your map for pure living. Hiding the Word in your heart is the best insurance you have against temptation. Remember when Satan was allowed to tempt Jesus in the wilderness? Read the story in Matthew 4:1-12. What was Jesus' reply to Satan?

Jesus quoted Scripture to ward off the temptations of Satan. It is helpful to memorize verses that will set up boundaries around areas where you are tempted. Then the Holy Spirit can speak to you through the verses when you need them most. Here are two examples of Scripture Boundaries.

For losing my temper . . .
Proverbs 14:17: "A quick-tempered man does foolish things"

Keeping my temper. . .
Proverbs 15:1: "A gentle answer turns away wrath, but a harsh word stirs up anger"

For feelings of worthlessness . . .
Luke 12: 6-7: " . . . The very hairs on your head are all numbered. Don't be afraid; you are worth more than many sparrows."

I am of great worth to God. . .
Romans 8:31: "If God is for us, who can be against us?"

What is an area of weakness in your Christian life with which you would like the Holy Spirit's help?

3 Using a concordance, topical Bible, or the help of a friend, choose two Scripture verses to be your "boundaries" of a godly path. Hide them in your heart so that you might not sin against God.

For _____ . . .

_____
_____
_____
_____
_____
_____
_____

Write out Galatians 5:25:

 As you walk in the Spirit, God promises to walk with you and protect you from the sins around you. A close walk with God, a good "accountability friend," and daily prayer are the needed ingredients for avoiding the flood of pain that would result from your sin.

4. Keep Your Foot from Evil

Read 2 Timothy 2:22. What are you to do when you experience evil desires?

The Bible says we are to flee from sin. Fleeing means running as fast as you can. The danger comes in thinking you are strong and can handle a situation, or that you are not vulnerable to sins, especially sins of the flesh. Don't flirt with temptation. Don't even get near it!

Read 1 Corinthians 10:13-14. What is the way of escape?

Purity in Marriage

The Lord God, the Holy One, the Righteous One, established the doctrine of sexual purity, and He has not changed. In 1 Corinthians 6:18-20 we read, "Flee from sexual immorality. All other sins a man commits are outside his body, but he who sins sexually sins against his own body. Do you not know that your body is a temple of the Holy Spirit, who is in you, whom you have received from God? You are not your own; you were bought at a price. Therefore honor God with your body."

What makes sexual purity especially important to God?

The words to the following song, written by Jon Mohr and recorded by Steve Green, are a powerful sermon about purity.

Guard Your Heart
by Jon Mohr

What appears to be a harmless glance
Can turn to romance
And homes are divided.
Feelings that should never have been
Awaken within
Tearing the heart in two,
Listen, I beg of you,

Guard your heart!
Guard your heart!
Don't trade it for treasure,
Don't give it away.

Guard your heart!
Guard your heart!
As payment for pleasure
It's a high price to pay,
For a soul that remains sincere
With a conscience clear,
Guard your heart

The human heart is easily swayed
And often betrayed
At the hand of emotion.
We dare not leave the outcome to chance,
We must choose in advance
Or live with the agony . . .
Such needless tragedy,
Guard your heart![1]

In the story of Joseph and Potiphar's wife in Genesis 39, we are taught a wonderful example of avoiding evil from the very start. Read Genesis 39:1-12. List all the things Joseph did to handle the situation with Potiphar's wife.

Write out Ephesians 4:26, 29-31:

Seldom do people fall into serious sin because they planned to do it. More often it begins with an unhappy or angry heart looking for satisfaction or by a small argument that gets out of hand. This is especially true of infidelity. Before we can even think about it, we are lost in sins that envelop us and unravel our lives.

Don't send your husband off to work with anger between you. It allows Satan the opportunity to jump in and stir up more strife. When sinful thoughts are allowed to creep in, they escalate. When your husband returns at night, you are likely to have thought and imagined all sorts of ideas that should never be. Determine to start each day instead with prayer for one another and a great send-off. Don't forget he's thinking all day, too. What do you want his thoughts of you to be?

The Lord demands purity and absolute faithfulness to our mates. Are there other ways that you can be unfaithful to your husband other than adultery? Give an example.

What about flirting? Is there such a thing as innocent flirting? Why do we usually flirt? How would flirting damage your marriage?

What about our appearance? Do we flirt with our clothing—the way we walk or sit? Why is this an important issue?

If you think flirting is innocent, how would you feel if your husband flirted?

Write out Hebrews 13:4:

You must be careful, as well, not to be responsible for hurting another marriage. You should treat every man you meet the way you would like other women to treat your husband!

The Rewards of Purity

Read Matthew 5:8. What are the rewards of purity?

Read Psalm 24:4-5. What are some examples of purity listed here? What can the pure person receive?

Your own personal purity will be a wonderful blessing to your children. When you model purity for your children, they receive a living example of modesty, truthfulness, and respect for God. Your daughters have a reliable model for presenting themselves (modesty in word and dress, etc.) and relating to men. And your children are shielded from the wrong books, magazines, television shows, movies, and videos, because you are honoring God with the choices you make for them and for yourself. By the time they are old enough to choose for themselves, they will know that "good, clean fun" really is fun!

Finally, because purity is "the moral excellence I demonstrate in my life as I consistently do what is right," your children will know they can depend upon you to do your best to act consistently. Children thrive on consistency!

May the Lord bless your decision to be pure in heart.

Prayer

Father, it is impossible for me to be pure without Your help. I want to honor You in my family, in my life. The world crashes in all around me with sights and sounds that appeal to my sinful nature.

Help me to come daily before You, an empty vessel needing and wanting to be filled by Your Spirit, grace, and, yes, mercy.

Thank You, Father, for Your perfect, sinless nature and that You can make me clean before Your eyes when I submit my will to Yours. I cannot do it alone. I love You, Lord. Amen.

For Further Reading

Elisabeth Elliot, *Passion and Purity* (Grand Rapids, Mich.: Fleming Revell, 1984).

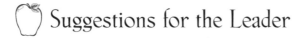

Suggestions for the Leader

 If time permits, have women share their Apple Seeds.

 Be sure women understand the importance of confession and repentance. Here are the steps to obtaining a clean heart as described in Psalm 51:

v.1 request for mercy

v. 7 request for cleansing

v. 10 request for a pure heart

v. 12 request for a willing spirit

God's forgiveness results in joy, witnessing, and praise:

v. 12 joy of God's salvation

v. 13 motivation to teach others about God's mercy

vs. 14-15 praise of God's righteousness

Invite the women to come to you or another mentor for help if they have not yet accepted Christ as their Savior.

 Some women may find their Scripture Boundaries too personal to share aloud. Others might want to share the verses they chose in order to be accountable. Offering to have these Scripture Boundaries made into little plaques or Bible bookmarks would be a thoughtful gift to remember this lesson. (Boundaries could be typed on a computer or written as calligraphy and then either placed in the small mats sold at craft stores, or backed with art board and laminated as a book-mark.) If a participant would like to have her Scripture Boundary made into such a gift, she should write the verses out as she would like them to appear. That way the typist needn't look up all the different Scripture verses, a time-consuming task.

4 If time permits, discuss what it means to "walk in the Spirit." Share a time you experienced the Spirit's protection in a temptation you have faced.

". . . Train the young women to love their husbands and children, to be sensible, chaste, domestic, kind, and submissive to their husbands, that the word of God may not be discredited." Titus 2:3–5 (RSV)

Lesson Six
Hospitality

Open up my heart, Father.
Fill me with Your love.
May Your Holy Spirit send me
Wisdom from above.
May my heart be warm and tender,
Give me eyes to see,
Open up my heart, O Lord.
Fill me with Your love.

Open up our home, Father.
Fill it with Your love.
May all those who enter
Feel Your presence from above.
Make it loving, safe, and warm
A shelter from the storm
Open up our home, O Lord,
Fill it with Your love.
—B. H.

Apple Seeds

Set the mood by singing "Open Up My Heart, Father" (music on p. 143).

Do you have a special memory of a time when someone opened his or her home to you? What do you remember most?

Apple Blossoms

The dictionary gives this definition of hospitality: friendly and generous reception and entertainment of guests. This description is remarkably comprehensive, because hospitality is cheerfully sharing food, shelter, and spiritual refreshment with those whom God brings into our lives. Attitude is an important part of the definition: we are to have generous spirits, and our guests should feel that we planned for them. In addition, they should feel entertained, which means to be occupied in a pleasant manner.

The idea of hospitality is a biblical one. Over and over again, God reminds His children to love strangers because they, too, were once strangers in a strange land (Deut. 10:18-19). Jesus often enjoyed the hospitality of His followers as He traveled from city to city. They welcomed Him, fed Him, and conversed with Him. They gave Him a much-needed break from the press of the crowds. He commended His hosts for their hospitality and blessed them. He desires fellowship with us.

Revelation 3:20 says, "Here I am! I stand at the door and knock. If anyone hears my voice and opens the door, I will come in and eat with him, and he with me." This verse is often used as an illustration of Christ knocking at your heart's door. He knocks first, but it is up to you to let Him into your heart. When you open your heart's door to Christ, you make yourself open and vulnerable to Him. He promises to come in!

Can you imagine Christ's knock at the door of your home? When you open the door, Jesus Christ is standing there. He asks you if He can come in. Would you be ready for Him? Would you feel presentable? Could you freely open the door and let Him into your home, or would you have to make excuses—for the state of your home, for the television program that is on, for the kind of magazines and books lying around. Remember that Christ always sees everything in your home, whether or not you hear Him knocking.

My friend Carol gave me a plaque that hangs in my kitchen. It says, "Invited or not, Jesus is present." It is a wonderful daily reminder that Jesus is here with me, He knows all about me, and He is still present! I love that thought. He desires to fellowship with me, even though I'm not perfect. Imagine that!

When Jesus comes to the door, He wants to stay for supper. And He has brought something to add to the meal. Sharing a meal together is an intimate occasion.

If Jesus came to dinner, you would use the best of everything you have—the best china, the prettiest tablecloth and flowers. You would serve your favorite and best-cooked meal, and do it with joy. You would do everything you knew how to make Jesus comfortable.

You can welcome the Lord into your home. Often Christians pray that Jesus be present at the table. He wants to be invited into your heart, and life, and home.

Read Matthew 25:25-40. How are you assured you will entertain Christ?

What do you expect from Christ when you invite Him into your home?

Write out Hebrews 13:1-2:

Wow! What do you think about that? Is your home ready for angels? Is the Lord (in the form of "the least of these brothers of mine") welcome in your home?

It is my hope this lesson will get you to the place where you can answer "Yes!" I want to calm some of your fears and show you the way to open your heart and home to others. Hospitality is sharing your home and yourself and being a servant to your family and guests. Being hospitable is being faithful and obedient to God. And as you treat others as you would treat the Lord, you will experience great joy!

Choice Fruit
Dedicate Your Home to God

A home can be described many ways. Circle the words that best describe your home.

Warm	Inviting	Messy	Neighborly	Open
Cold	Happy	Sad	Cordial	Tense
Unfriendly	Loving	Cozy	Spontaneous	Angry
Fragrant	Formal	Casual	Structured	Sterile

Regardless of how it is now, with God's help, your home can become a home of hospitality.

Read Psalm 127:1. How do you think God builds a house?

How could God be more central to the day-to-day building of your home?

Begin by dedicating your home to God. You may want to have a ceremony in which you prayerfully and joyfully dedicate your home and everything in it to God. By dedicating your home to God, you are affirming that all that you have is a gift from His almighty hand. It is not yours to hold onto; it is meant to share with others and minister to them.

Read Psalm 50:9-12. In verse 12, what does God say belongs to Him?

Knowing everything belongs to God, what would be a meaningful way to dedicate your home to God?

If our homes are dedicated to God, how would that affect the following situations?

• A friend's son wants to stay behind while his parents do a two-week missions project in Mexico . . .

• A pint-sized dinner guest scratches the diningroom table . . .

• The college pastor mentions a record number of international students enrolled at the nearby college—many lonely and craving American friends . . .

• An older man at church is unexpectedly widowed . . .

• A new trumpet player in the family could have been Joshua's secret weapon to topple the walls of Jericho . . .

• The house is a mess when a next-door neighbor stops by in need of advice . . .

• While you plan the menu for Thanksgiving dinner, a single woman who often sits for your kids keeps coming to mind . . .

Sometimes we can be enslaved by our homes and possessions. We become too concerned with the impressions our homes will make on others. Or we worry too much that things might get broken if we, or our children, entertain. We forget that the most important thing is to use our homes and possessions for their intended purpose, which is to share the love of Christ with others. But when we become aware that everything belongs to God, we can entertain with attitudes of thankfulness and joy! It is very freeing!

Write out 1 John 3:17-18:

Showing Hospitality to My Own Family

Before your home can feel comfortable to strangers and friends, it needs to feel comfortable for your own family. What kind of welcome does your husband receive at the end of the day? What kind of welcome do your children receive when they return from school? What will be their memories of home? Ask your family where they are most comfortable in your home. What makes that room or area their favorite spot?

Take an objective look at your home. Is it inviting? Comfortable? Make the changes that are necessary to make it better, such as moving the furniture around, providing a good reading lamp, or adding some pretty accessories.

A few changes I could make are:

What are your memories of your childhood home?

If your memories are positive, reinvent them in your home. If your childhood memories are troublesome to you, be determined, with the help of God, to make wonderful memories for your children.

Write out 1 Peter 4:9:

Though this verse applies to all who enter our homes, we sometimes grumble more to family members. Hospitality is not just food and drink—it is the essence of kindness, submission, and generosity within our homes.

What are some practical ways to show hospitality to your family?

It is difficult to make your home feel inviting to friends unless it feels inviting to your family.

Hospitality—A Shared Priority

Read 1 Timothy 3:2 and Titus 1:8. What is required of men in church leadership?

Why do you think hospitality was part of the list? How would hospitality impact a man's ministry?

Hospitality needs to be a shared priority in a Christian home because it is a command to both spouses equally. Sit down with your spouse and decide, generally, how you want to offer hospitality:

"Are we most comfortable with being spontaneous or planning in advance?"

If you are going to open your home to people spontaneously (for instance, after first meeting them at church), you and your husband need to be in agreement. If you invite without asking what plans your spouse has for the day, your guests may feel the tension in your home between you and your spouse. Agree beforehand that you will ask each other first if it is a convenient day to have guests and if you are prepared at home. If the answer is "no," you can plan for another day or consider going out for a sandwich or dessert.

How we would like to incorporate hospitality into our family life:

"Are there specific persons or types of people God has placed on our hearts?"

Besides being open to whomever God sends your way, you might feel called to invite, for instance, new families in church, couples in your neighborhood, refugee families, or international students. You might feel called to the challenges of offering long-term help, for instance, to a friend experiencing health problems.

Because we have a child with Down's syndrome, we really appreciate friends who are sensitive to his needs, but also to ours, and invite him to their home for a day, a dinner, or a swim in their pool. Our friends the Topps, and their entire family, include Mark in various activities with them, giving us a break. Today Mark lives in a group home, and the Topps now minister not only to Mark, but to all his friends with whom he lives. Many friends have helped us over the years; the Topps are but one wonderful example.

Do you know a parent who could use a break from a special-needs child? Do you have a friend who is caring for a parent and needs a much-needed break? This is hospitality at its best!

People who might enjoy our hospitality:

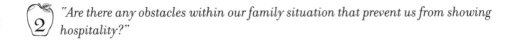 *"Are there any obstacles within our family situation that prevent us from showing hospitality?"*

Brainstorm ways to overcome them. There is a Chinese proverb: "If I keep a green bough in my heart, the singing bird will come." If you have a willing heart, God will bring opportunities for you to open your heart during those times you cannot open your home.

Obstacles we need to overcome:

Once your goals are established, you might want to divide up the tasks to accomplish your goals, according to interest, ability, and practicality. Even if you choose to do the cooking (to try out recipes you learned in Apples of Gold?), there are many ways your husband can share in preparing to entertain. And when the guests arrive, he can greet the guests at the door with you. He can offer an appetizer or drink to your guests while you finish tossing the salad, for example.

If you have shouldered most of the task of entertaining in the past, don't assume your husband knows what needs to be done. Describe what goes into an evening, and suggest ways he could be most helpful. When your husband knows what to expect, he will be better able to do his part. Don't wait until the last minute to discuss the evening; you will both be frustrated.

Read Acts 28:7-10. What might have made Paul's visit inconvenient for his host?

This is a household that truly understands hospitality. Publius, the homeowner, welcomed Paul's entourage for three days. They were entertained hospitably even though Publius was also caring for his father, who was sick in bed. Then when Paul prayed for him and he was healed, the rest of the sick on the island came to the house as well. This was a busy place. To top it off, when Paul's group left, they were furnished with supplies. What a selfless example of hospitality!

Hospitality to New Friends

Read 3 John 1, 5-8. To whom did John write this letter?

For what is the man commended?

Write out Romans 16:23:

Both John and Paul commend Gaius for his hospitality. Imagine offering hospitality to the whole church, old friends and newcomers alike! That is a lot of hospitality!

There is a saying that strangers are just friends we have not met. Some of the greatest times of hospitality we have shared in our home were with brand new friends.

Every week visitors come to church for the first time. From time to time, get a list of those people from your church office, and invite a few to Sunday dinner or a picnic. Sometimes you meet new friends sitting near you in church. Consider inviting them home with you or make arrangements for a future date.

My husband, Lee, and I have been doing this for many years. Sometimes, years later, someone will come up to us and tell us how much the invitation to our home meant to them when they were new at church.

Making new friends is a great joy, and people will love being invited to your home, even if you order in pizza, or just have dessert and coffee. It truly is the fellowship that counts.

Our first home was very small—just four rooms. We did not have a dining room, but we still loved to be with our friends. On one occasion, we invited about twelve friends for a taco party. I placed a large tablecloth on the floor and used red-and-white check paper plates and napkins. We all sat in a circle and had a wonderful time. It doesn't have to be fancy to be fun.

Write out Romans 12:13:

Reread the scenarios under Dedicate Your Home to God. Do you know someone with a deep need for your hospitality? Someone who is hurting? Sick? Lonely? Struggling financially? Share your home and love with them.

The Blessings of Hospitality

How far are you willing to go to obey God's command to be hospitable?

Your hospitality will have far-reaching blessings!

For instance, as you share your home with others, your children will see wonderful lessons in giving. If you invite missionaries and guest speakers, your children can learn much about the mission field during these up-close and personal encounters. Helping people who are more challenged financially will help your children appreciate all they have. And when you entertain friends who have more of this world's good than you have, your children will see that people are people, and we all need to learn from one another. It's important to remember that sometimes those who have more are lonely because people do not invite them to their homes. Your children will come to understand that God has given you all you have, and it is right for you. They needn't be ashamed of their home or what they have.

And even if you never entertain "angels unawares," you will someday hear, "'Whatever you did for one of the least of these brothers of mine, you did for me'" (Matt. 25:40).

Prayer

Our precious Heavenly Father, giver of all we enjoy, we thank You. We dedicate our homes and families to You.

Help us to freely share our home, and to welcome strangers and friends alike. Make this home a place where our children will dwell happily, where great memories are made, and where delicious food is shared.

Make it a place where laughter rings out, where family and friends find comfort and refuge, where hurts can be shared freely and healed by Your gracious hand.

Help me to take that first step, Lord—to put aside my fears of failure and to trust Your faithfulness to help me. Make me a servant eager to do Your will in the lives of others. Amen.

Practical Hospitality

What are some important things you feel need to happen before you are ready to entertain? The ideal is a home that is more or less ever ready. The home that is organized can receive guests more readily. You will be more ready to invite someone to your home if you feel good about it. This does not mean perfection in your home! It does mean that it is picked up, that the bathrooms are clean and have fresh towels, and that your home feels comfortable to your guests.

What is keeping you from practicing hospitality?

Whatever is keeping you from being hospitable must change if you desire to honor this admonition from the Lord.

If you need help getting your home organized, ask a well-organized friend for advice. How does she do it? What method does she use?

Pick up some habits that will help you keep your home in order:

• It is more motivating to maintain a home you enjoy. Decide how to make it more appealing to your senses. Then go to work. Take a room at a time, rearranging it to better suit your family's needs. Move the furniture, rearrange pictures, add some flowers.

• Before you go to bed at night, take a walk through the living areas of your house, picking up newspapers, toys, and other things that are out of place. You will feel so much better about your home in the morning.

• Get up early enough for "you time." Even if you are not a morning person, you will feel better about yourself all day if you shower, comb your hair, brush your teeth, and get dressed.

• Make the beds as soon as you get up. Teach your children how to properly make their beds, and expect them to do it.

• Do the dishes as soon as you finish a meal. A clean kitchen is not only a wonderful feeling, it is necessary for your family's health. It is much more enjoyable to prepare the next meal in a clean kitchen.

• Clean as you go. Don't let things pile up.

• Keep up with the laundry. Fold a load as soon as you empty the dryer. It will help you not to feel overwhelmed with folding.

• Vacuum and dust as needed. A quick dusting can make your entire house feel clean.

• Ask for help! Don't complain about all you have to do. Children—even young ones—can and should help with the house. Share duties with your husband, but play fair! Make a system that works for you and stick to it!

• Some things need to be done daily, others weekly, and some less often. What do you need to do to have an orderly home? Plan it.

• Expect occasional "fun breaks." If something wonderful comes along to do with your family or a friend, do it from time to time with no guilt. An occasionally messy house will do no harm!

Come on Over!

• Make a guest list. Call or jot a note inviting your guests. Be sure they know what to expect: what to wear, what time to arrive, if children are invited, and so on.

• If you are sending invitations, be sure to ask for a reply. If you do not receive a reply within a reasonable time, it is acceptable to call for a response.

• It is also fine to be spontaneous and invite people over on the same day you want them to come. Examples include a picnic on a beautiful day, or soup around the fire. Some of your best parties will be on those occasions.

• It isn't hard to keep a complete "loaves and fishes meal" on hand for spontaneous hospitality. If you have the freezer space, you can store a special box holding a casserole that can be put in the oven frozen, bread sticks that bake at the same temperature, vegetables, a package of balled fruit, and a cake that freezes well, such as pound cake, or those special cookies your extended family looks forward to having at your house. Promise yourself you won't dip into these emergency rations unless you can replenish them immediately. You won't feel the need to touch the "loaves and fishes box" if you get in the habit of making "one for tonight and one for the freezer" whenever you make casseroles or bake desserts.

Invitation Accepted

• As the party day approaches, head for your front door. It is your home's first impression. What is it? Clean the windows, sweep the steps, add flowers in summer and a wreath in winter. Lights on, no burned-out bulbs!

• Have a place for coats, boots, and umbrellas.

• Put a big helping of warmth in your welcome. If appropriate, give a hug. Keep the focus on your guests, not on you.

• Be interested in your guests. How are they? If they are new to you, be sure to ask them the correct pronunciation of their names, or even the spelling. It helps you to remember. Use name tags for large groups. It helps everyone.

• Offer them a seat. Some people will not sit down until they are offered a seat. If you are planning a beverage, offer it to them at this time.

• It is up to the host and hostess to make sure that the guests remain comfortable. Keep the conversation going.

• Have dinner ready on time. If your guests are invited to a seven o'clock dinner, be sure that dinner is served no later than seven thirty. An on-time dinner can only happen if you are well organized. It is not polite to make guests wait for dinner.

• Offer an appetizer while they wait.

• If you need to be busy in the kitchen, your husband and family can keep things going for a short time.

The Meal

• When you plan a dinner party, decide your menu well in advance of the event. Keep the menu manageable so that you can enjoy your guests. Shop early in the week. Be sure that you write your shopping list from your menu, so that you don't have to run back to the store for things you forgot. Shopping for things you forgot to buy takes precious time.

• Remember that a nice salad, a beautiful casserole, fresh rolls, and dessert make a great party. You do not need many different kinds of food for a successful evening. It should, however, be delicious!

• Think about the textures and colors of the foods you select. For instance, if you are serving chicken, a green vegetable will be prettier to serve with it than corn.

• Decide if the dinner will be served family style (bowls on the table), if you will serve up each plate, or if it is a buffet. Be sure to have serving pieces ready for a buffet or family style. If you plate your dinner in the kitchen, you may need a helper to get everything to the table at once. Enlist the help of a child, your husband, or a guest.

• Make a list of things that need to be done before the party. Keep it handy and refer to it often. Make a plan. Keep to it.

• Set the table early in the day or the day before. When the house is ready ahead of time, you will not be so frustrated in the kitchen. Don't wait until the last minute to iron your tablecloth or napkins.

• Be sure to have candles and matches ready. (Remember: no candles during the day.)

• Check the salt and pepper. You don't want to take the time to fill salt and pepper shakers after guests arrive.

• If you are unsure about how to set your table properly, save up for a book on etiquette. It will be a great help for you in all areas of entertaining. (This would be a great bridal shower gift!)

• Get dressed early! Don't wait until the last minute. You will be frazzled and unsure of yourself. Give yourself some time for you!

• Clean up minimally in the kitchen, and then enjoy your guests. It is uncomfortable for your guests if you are working the entire time they are in your home, and you will not enjoy the evening.

Entertaining Guests

• Entertaining does not mean that you need to plan a program and sing for your guests, although singing praise choruses is our favorite way to complete an evening of fellowship in our home. It does mean, I believe, you can occupy your guests in a pleasant manner because you have given thought to the evening. It helps to know something about your guests and be interested in knowing more. Study up on your guests ahead of time. This will help you plan topics or activities with their interests in mind. Find out:

—What are their interests?

—What are their jobs?

—Do they have children? How many? What ages?

—What hobbies do they have?

• Try to envision any needs your guests might have. Do they need encouragement? Relaxation? A listening ear? A chance to have fun?

• If you're having over a busy young family, you might even designate one of your children as a "mother's helper" (or hire one) to amuse the children while the parents enjoy some "just adults" time with you.

• Plan a few key questions to ask at dinner to encourage good sharing. Try to base them on your guests' interests and needs. Start a "Good Question Collection," such as, "If you could have dinner with anyone, whom would it be with? Why?"

• Make some simple plans for the evening. Have a game ready for after dinner, or plan to take a walk, if your guests like the idea. Make your guests feel at ease; encourage them to sit in your most "comfy" chair, maybe even "your" chair. What does your family enjoy doing? Share that with your guests.

Overnight Guests

Be sure the room your guests will occupy is ready and clean when they arrive. Check out the entire room—floors, windows, woodwork. Make it as nice as you possibly can.

The Guest Bedroom

• Consider ironing the sheets. Make the bed as pretty and comfortable as possible. How are the pillows? Some people like small pillows, some fluffy. If possible, have one of each. Are the blankets clean? Details are important here—more so than in the rest of the house. Make your guests feel special.

• Be sure there is a good light in the room for reading in bed. Sometimes guests have a hard time getting to sleep in a strange place. Place a good book and a couple of current magazines in the room.

• Flowers are wonderful. Even a single flower in a pretty vase will do nicely.

• Place a chair in the bedroom if you have room for one.

• A mirror is nice to have in the room, especially if the guests are sharing a bathroom with your family or other guests.

The Bathroom

• Clean the shower or tub. Be sure there is no hair anywhere!

• Clean the toilet thoroughly.

• Be sure there is a good bar of soap, shampoo, and some fluffy, clean towels and washcloths.

• Provide a good hand mirror so guests can see the back of their hair.

• Buy a new toothbrush in case your guests forget.

Courtesy to Guests

• If guests are staying a few days, ask them what they like for breakfast, if they have any food dislikes or allergies, if they prefer coffee or tea, and if there is anything that will help them feel more at home.

 If you like, tell your guests to help themselves to a drink, sandwich, or whatever they would like.

When You Are a Guest

• When hosts invite you to their home, they are offering you a time in their place of peace and sanctuary. It is an honor to be invited into someone's home for dinner. Treat it like an honor.

- Be on time.
- Leave problems behind. (Your hosts deserve your best!)
- Know what you are expected to wear.
- Bring a small hostess gift. (Even a single flower or some candy is appropriate. It need not be expensive. It is the courtesy that counts.)
- Send a thank-you note.

The Party's Over; It's Time to Call It a Day . . .

And finally, your bedroom!

- Your bedroom is your private sanctuary. What does it look and feel like?
- If possible, keep your bedroom just that—a place of rest, retreat, and refuge for you and your husband.
- Try to keep it from being a multi-purpose room—a study, storage room, and so on. Don't let clothes and other items accumulate in the room.
- Make your bed as beautiful as you can. Splurge on pretty sheets, and keep them fresh and smelling wonderful! Have a good light next to each side of the bed for reading.
- Buy a lock for your bedroom door if it does not have one. You need privacy in your marriage, even if it is just to retreat and talk or to get dressed. You will be far more relaxed if you know a child will not be barging in on you. Children can easily be taught to respect your privacy. Teach them to knock on the door if they really need you.
- If you treat it as such, your bedroom will become a haven, your special place, a place you look forward to going to at the end of a long, busy day.

May hospitality become your joy!

For Further Reading

Letitia Baldrige, *The Amy Vanderbilt Complete Book of Etiquette* (New York: Doubleday, 1978).

Dolley Carlson, *Gifts from the Heart* (Colorado Springs, Colo.: Chariot Victor Publishing, 1998).

Terry Willits, *Creating a SenseSational Home* (Grand Rapids, Mich.: Zondervan Publishing House, 1996).

Suggestions for the Leader

1 If time permits, have a few women share their answers to the Apple Seeds question. Be prepared to share a story of your own.

2 One woman whose door is always open says, "Showing hospitality isn't always convenient." Invite women to share their struggles with hospitality. Have the group brainstorm solutions.

3 Demonstrate how to put together a Guest Room Basket. Many guests are reluctant to ask for the things they need, or you might not be around to provide them. That's why it's nice to have a Guest Room Basket that anticipates their desires. To make one, gather these items and keep them in a reclosable plastic bag. Before guests arrive, arrange the items in an attractive basket. These ideas will get you started:

- Extra toothbrushes
- Sample-size tube of toothpaste
- Dental floss
- Travel-size deodorant
- Comb
- Disposable shavers
- Individually wrapped sanitary napkins
- Tampons
- Cough drops
- Band-Aids
- Pain reliever (or, if children are around, instructions where to find medications and first-aid supplies)
- Travel-size moisturizer
- Stain pretreating stick (to use before an item is repacked in the suitcase)
- Pencil and pad
- Stamped postcards from your town, or even a fun family picture backed as a postcard
- Brochures from local attractions, in case guests have time to visit
- Local map to borrow

Table Talk Questions

Each week the mentors at each luncheon table will facilitate a Table Talk discussion. It is up to the mentors to keep the discussion on target. Table Talk helps everyone feel included at the table. It takes the lesson for the day to completion.

Kindness

- Think about your neighborhood. Go around the area in your mind. Does anyone come to mind to whom you can show kindness this week?
- If you were going to write a "thanks for all your kindness" note to someone, who would it be? Why?
- Share an act of kindness that you did for someone.
- What part does kindness play in evangelism? What can we do to attract the unbeliever to Christ?
- Is there something you are doing—or would like to do—that would attract others to Christ?
- What part of this lesson is especially meaningful to you?

Loving Your Husband

- Everyone loves a love story. Do you have a good story to share?
- The five needs most men identify are: sexual fulfillment, recreational companionship, an attractive spouse, domestic support, and admiration. How do you meet your husband's needs? Where could you improve?
- Is it obvious to others that you truly love your husband? Why?
- How do you pamper your husband?
- Is there any part of this lesson that is especially meaningful to you?

Loving Your Children

- What makes you think your children are secure in your love?
- How do you tell them and show them daily that you love them?
- What nighttime rituals add security to your children's lives?
- What does your family do for fun?
- What is the most difficult part of parenting for you?
- How can the mentors of Apples of Gold help you?
- How do you want to be remembered by your children when they are grown?
- What part of this lesson is especially meaningful to you?

Submission

- Is it difficult for you to submit to authority? To your husband? Why?
- Who makes the majority of decisions in your marriage?
- How does submission to God and your husband enhance your marriage?
- What happens when the two of you have differing opinions and plans?
- Have you ever made a respectful appeal to your husband concerning a decision (similar to the process Daniel used)? What happened?
- Was there a time you submitted to your husband's decision and God used it in a wonderful way? Tell about it.
- What part of this lesson is especially meaningful to you?

Purity

- When do you feel the most vulnerable to temptation?
  —When you are too busy?
  —When you want more attention?
  —When you need more romance?
  —At other times?
- How does your family handle the problem of TV, magazines, and other impure influences that are all around?
- Children need to learn early that their bodies belong to the Lord. How can you teach purity to your sons and daughters?
- Are you comfortable talking about purity with your spouse? With your children? What would make it easier?
- What part of this lesson is especially meaningful to you?

Hospitality

- What is your favorite way to show hospitality?
- What is the best memory of hospitality shown to you?
- What frightens you the most about entertaining in your home?
- Is there any part of this lesson that is especially meaningful to you?
- How will Apples of Gold change the way you entertain?

The Menus

Italian Dinner

Bruschetta Appetizer
Minestrone Soup
Caesar Salad with Homemade Croutons
Penne Pasta with Red Sauce and Cheese
Springtime Spaghetinni
Country Herb Flatbread
Tuscan Almond Torte

Bruschetta Appetizer

Olive Paste
1 cup pitted ripe olives
2 teaspoons balsamic vinegar
2 cloves garlic
1 teaspoon capers
1 tablespoon olive oil

Combine olives, vinegar, garlic, capers, and olive oil in blender or processor. Cover and blend or process until smooth, running a spatula down sides of bowl halfway through. Put in airtight container for up to 2 days, if desired.

Tomato Topping
2 medium tomatoes (can use red and yellow), chopped
1/3 cup green onion, chopped
1 tablespoon olive oil
1 tablespoon Italian seasoning
1/8 teaspoon pepper

Stir chopped tomatoes, chopped green onions, olive oil, Italian seasoning, and pepper together. Put in airtight container for up to 2 days.

Toasts

1 loaf Italian bread
2 tablespoons olive oil

Slice bread into 1/4-inch slices. Brush with olive oil and put on ungreased cookie sheet. Bake at 425 degrees until lightly browned, about 5 minutes.

To Assemble:

Spread each piece of toast with thin layer of olive paste. Top with 2 tablespoons tomato mixture. Sprinkle with Parmesan cheese, and bake at 425 degrees for 2-3 minutes.

Minestrone Soup

1/3 cup olive oil
1 large onion
4 large carrots
2 large potatoes, diced
1 green pepper, diced
3 medium zucchini, diced
1 cup green beans, cut
1 medium cabbage, shredded
5 cups beef stock (see "Begin with a Good Stock" on p. 121)
5 cups chicken stock
1 can plum tomatoes
2 tablespoons oregano
1 tablespoon basil
salt and pepper to taste
outer rind of a 2-inch piece of Parmesan cheese
1 1/2 cups white beans
1 can kidney beans
1 pound cheese-stuffed tortellini
1 1/2 pounds sweet Italian sausage, cut into 1 1/2 inch pieces
3 tablespoons sugar
Parmesan cheese

Sauté onion in oil in large stockpot 10-15 minutes over medium heat. Stir in carrots, and sauté 3 more minutes. Add potatoes, green pepper, zucchini, and green beans, cooking each vegetable 2-3 minutes before adding more. When all vegetables have been added, stir in cabbage and cook five minutes more. Add stocks, tomatoes with juice, oregano, basil, salt and pepper to taste, and sugar.

Bury cheese in the middle of soup. Heat to boiling, reduce heat, and simmer covered over low heat about 3 hours. The soup will be very thick.

Stir in beans and tortellini. Raise heat to cook tortellini, but stir often to prevent tortellini from sticking to bottom. Stir in cooked sausage. Simmer another twenty to thirty minutes. Ladle into shallow bowl and garnish lavishly with Parmesan cheese.

Caesar Salad with Homemade Croutons

1/3 cup lemon juice
1/3 cup olive oil
1 egg
1 tablespoon olive oil to rub inside salad bowl
1/4 teaspoon salt
1 clove garlic, minced
2 tomatoes, sliced in eighths
Romaine lettuce
1/2 cup Parmesan cheese
1/2 pound bacon, cooked crisp and crumbled
1/3 cup green onion, chopped
2 anchovies, chopped (optional)
1/2 teaspoon pepper
1 1/4 teaspoon oregano
1 cup homemade croutons (recipe below)

Mix juice with oil. Cover egg in shell with water in a pan. Bring to boil, remove from heat. Let stand for one minute. Remove from water and refrigerate. Rub wooden salad bowl with olive oil and sprinkle with salt. Then rub garlic around inside of bowl.

Place sliced tomatoes in bottom of bowl. Wash Romaine lettuce thoroughly, drying it between paper towels. Break lettuce into bit-sized pieces and put into bowl. Sprinkle with Parmesan cheese, bacon, green onions, anchovies, pepper, oregano, and croutons. Remove softly cooked egg from shell. Add egg to lemon juice and olive oil mixture. Blend. Add to salad just before serving, tossing well. (I like to toss salad with my very clean hands, or wear disposable plastic gloves.)

Croutons

1/4 cup butter, melted
1/4 cup olive oil
1 small loaf French or sourdough bread, sliced
garlic salt

Mix butter and olive oil in bowl. Slice French bread (or other heavy-textured bread, such as sourdough) into 1-inch slices. Brush with butter-and-oil mixture on both sides. Sprinkle generously with garlic salt. Bake in 400-degree oven, watching carefully until nicely browned and crisped, turning once. Remove from oven, cool, and then cut into 1-inch cubes.

These are so yummy! They are nothing like the ones you buy in a bag at the store and are well worth the few minutes to make.

Penne Pasta with Red Sauce and Cheese

6 tablespoons olive oil

1 1/2 cups onion, chopped

1 teaspoon chopped garlic

2 28-ounce cans crushed tomatoes, drained

2 teaspoons basil

1/2 teaspoon crushed red pepper

1/4 cup sugar

2 cups chicken stock (see "Begin with a Good Stock" on p. 121)

1 pound pasta, Penne or Rigatoni

2 1/2 cups Havarti cheese, grated

1 red pepper, roasted, peeled, and chopped

1/3 cup Kalamata olives, pitted

1/3 cup Parmesan cheese, grated

2 teaspoons basil, fresh or dried

1/4 cup fresh basil (optional)

Heat 3 tablespoons olive oil in heavy stockpot over medium heat. Add onion and garlic. Sauté until translucent, about 5 minutes. Mix in tomatoes, 2 teaspoons basil, roasted red pepper, and sugar. Bring to boil, add broth. Bring to boil again.

Reduce heat to medium. Simmer until mixture is reduced to 6 cups, stirring occasionally (about 70 minutes). Season with salt and pepper.

Cook and drain pasta. Put pasta in greased casserole (10" x 15"), stir in olives and roasted red pepper. Cover with sauce and cheeses. Bake at 350 degrees for 25 minutes. Serve with additional Parmesan if desired. Garnish with 1/4 cup fresh basil, if desired.

To Roast a Red Pepper:

Cut red pepper in half. Remove seeds. Place under broiler of oven, or on grill. Broil or grill until blackened all over (watch carefully and turn when it blackens). Put pepper in plastic bag and let stand until skin is wrinkled all over and cooled (about 20 more minutes). Skin will easily peel off. Chop.

Springtime Spaghetinni

2 tablespoons salt
1 pound thin noodles
1/4 cup butter
2 teaspoons minced garlic
3 large carrots, julienned
1 medium zucchini, julienned
1 small red pepper, julienned
1 cup whipping cream
1/2 cup Parmesan cheese, grated
1/2 teaspoon nutmeg
1/2 teaspoon salt
1/4 teaspoon pepper
1/2 teaspoon dried dill (optional)
additional Parmesan cheese as garnish (optional)

Cook pasta according to package directions. Drain. Melt butter, add garlic, and sauté until it begins to color (about 1 minute). Add vegetables, and toss over high heat for 3 minutes. Remove from heat. When burner is cooled, place vegetables back over stove over medium heat. Stir in cream, Parmesan cheese, and nutmeg. Add salt and pepper to taste. Add pasta to skillet, and toss gently to blend well. Garnish with dill, if desired. Pass additional cheese.

This is a delicious vegetarian main dish, but if you like, for each guest add a chicken breast prepared your favorite way. Or add 2 cups of cubed, cooked chicken to pasta.

Country Herb Flatbread

1 10-ounce Pillsbury Refrigerated Pizza Crust
4 1/2 teaspoons olive oil
2 teaspoons dried Herbes de Provence (or mix 1/2 teaspoon each of thyme, marjoram, rosemary, and basil leaves)
6 oil-packed sun-dried tomatoes, drained and chopped
1/3 cup Chèvre (goat cheese), softened
2 eggs
dash pepper

Heat oven to 400 degrees. Spray 13" x 9" pan with cooking spray. Unroll dough. Place on sprayed pan. Starting at center, press dough with hands, making indentations over surface of dough with fingers. Brush with 3 teaspoons of the oil. Sprinkle with herbs and tomatoes.

In medium bowl, combine cheeses, eggs, remaining oil, and remaining herbs. With wire whisk, mix well. Pour evenly over tomatoes, spreading carefully. Bake at 400 degrees for 15-20 minutes, until edges are golden brown. Cut into squares.

—Nancy Gerhard

Tuscan Almond Torte

1 cup sugar
1 cup almond paste
1/4 cup butter, room temperature
4 eggs
1 teaspoon vanilla
1 cup flour
1 teaspoon baking powder
1/2 cup whipping cream
4 ounces Marscarpone cheese
individual chocolate bar, shaved
1/2 cup toasted, sliced almonds

Beat sugar, almond paste, and butter in a large mixing bowl with an electric mixer on low speed till blended. Beat in eggs and vanilla till smooth. Sprinkle flour and baking powder atop; beat just till combined. Pour into a greased and floured 9-inch springform pan.

Bake in a 325-degree oven for 50-55 minutes, or till a toothpick inserted near center comes out clean. Cool in pan on a wire rack for 10 minutes. Loosen cake from sides of pan. Cool completely on rack. Remove sides of pan.

Chill mixing bowl and beaters. Right before serving, beat whipping cream in the chilled bowl just till soft peaks form. Stir Marscarpone cheese; fold into whipped cream.

To serve, transfer cake to a serving platter. Mound whipping cream mixture atop cake. Garnish with shaved chocolate and toasted almonds.

Make-ahead directions: Seal cake in an airtight container. Cover and freeze up to 6 months. Thaw frozen cake in the refrigerator overnight. Let stand approximately 1 hour at room temperature before serving. Garnish cake as directed.

All-American Dinner

Chicken Rice Soup
Tossed Salad with Lemon Dressing
Family Favorite Beef Roast
Corn Pudding
Grammy's Wonderful Rolls
Fresh Green Beans Steamed Until Just Tender
Apple Pastry Bars

Chicken Rice Soup

1 whole chicken
6 cups chicken stock (homemade or broth)
1 bunch celery
1 bunch (about 8) green onions
7 large carrots, whole
salt and pepper to taste
1 tablespoon prepared mustard
3/4 cup rice, uncooked
2 tablespoons parsley

Wash chicken thoroughly. Put into stockpot with broth. Cook on stove top, bring to boil; then simmer until the chicken falls from bone (approximately 1 hour). Cook with 2 stalks celery, and 3 carrots, whole.

Remove chicken, celery, and carrots to a colander. Cool and remove all chicken from bones.

Put 2 cups of picked chicken back into stock pot with broth. (Put remaining chicken in sealed containers or bags for use in sandwiches, salads, or casseroles. This is much healthier than store-bought cold cuts, which may have harmful additives. It is also a budget cutter.) Cut all remaining celery into pieces, your size choice, and remaining carrots, cut into similar-sized pieces. Add mustard, and taste broth. Add salt and pepper to taste. (IF YOUR BROTH IS NOT RICH AND

TASTY, YOUR SOUP WILL NOT BE DELICIOUS). Add rice and parsley, and simmer until rice is cooked.

Begin with a Good Stock:

Use the method just described to prepare your own stock. Cook a whole chicken with 3 stalks of celery, 2 carrots, and 1 medium onion, if desired. Cook in 6 cups of homemade chicken broth (or canned chicken broth). Add salt and pepper to taste and 1 tablespoon of mustard. Remove chicken, and strain broth. Broth can be kept in refrigerator in covered glass jars for up to a week. Use cooked chicken for salads, sandwiches, and so on. Beef stock will be made the same way, but starting with beef soup bones or a small chuck roast. Add the seasonings you love, such as basil, rosemary, or tarragon. ALL GOOD COOKS SHOULD LEARN TO MAKE WONDERFUL STOCKS. Experiment with different seasonings. Always start with a small amount of seasoning and add more if needed. The flavors intensify as they cook.

Tossed Salad with Lemon Dressing

Salad

greens of your choice (such as Boston, Romaine, and red leaf lettuce or spinach)

vegetables of your choice (such as cucumber, tomato, red or green onion, etc., cut up)

Lemon Dressing

1/2 cup salad oil
1/4 cup lemon juice
3 tablespoons tarragon vinegar
2 tablespoons sugar
2 tablespoons minced green onion
1 teaspoon salt
1/4 teaspoon dry mustard
dash pepper

Combine all dressing ingredients in a jar with tight-fitting lid, preferably glass. (I save mayonnaise jars for this purpose.) Shake well and let stand until ingredients are well blended. Refrigerate, if desired. (This dressing is a true favorite of mine. My friends all seem to like it as well. The ingredients are usually on hand, and the flavor is delicate, showing off the greens.)

Family Favorite Beef Roast

(This smells so delicious while roasting that by the time it is done, your family will be very hungry!)

2 tablespoons olive oil, for browning
one 3-4 pound beef chuck or blade roast
1 large onion
carrots, desired amount

Sauce
2 tablespoons flour
4 tablespoons brown sugar
2 tablespoons prepared mustard, Dijon style
1 tablespoon Worcestershire Sauce
1 teaspoon salt
1 cup ketchup

Brown meat on all sides in heavy pot in small amount of olive oil. Put a sheet of heavy duty aluminum foil on a baking sheet. (It is important to use the large sheet of foil and be sure it is the heavy duty variety.) You may need two overlapping sheets, but be sure to seal pieces together. Put browned beef on foil; slice onion over top. Peel carrots and slice on the diagonal into large chunks, approximately 1 1/2 inches in length. Put as many as you like atop beef. Mix sauce ingredients together, and pour over beef. Wrap carefully; avoid making any tears in the foil. Bake at 350 degrees until completely tender, about 4 hours, depending on size and thickness of your roast. Open foil and serve. You can also cook meat in an oven cooking bag.

Corn Pudding

2 large cans cream-style corn, undrained
1 large can whole kernel corn
1 box Jiffy Corn Bread Mix
1 stick butter or margarine
1 tablespoon flour
2 tablespoons sugar
1/2 teaspoon salt
3 eggs, beaten
1 cup milk
Swiss cheese, sliced or grated to thoroughly cover pudding

Mix all ingredients except Swiss cheese together in bowl. Put in greased 9" x 13" casserole. Bake at 350 degrees until just set in middle. (When you wiggle pan, center of pudding should not move.) Do not overbake. Top with Swiss cheese and bake a few minutes more until cheese is just melted. Cool slightly. Cut in squares.

Grammy's Wonderful Rolls

We could always count on having these delicious rolls when we ate at Mom Huizenga's home. Made larger, they are wonderful hamburger buns. It took me a while to learn how to make these, to have a good feel for working with dough, but it is well worth the effort! Try not to add too much additional flour. It will make the finished product dry and heavy. Keep dough slightly sticky.

1/2 cup sugar
3 packages yeast
2 teaspoons salt
6 cups flour
1 stick butter, melted
2 cups lukewarm water
1 egg

Combine sugar, yeast, salt, and flour. Heat butter and water to lukewarm. Add to flour mix, and beat well until smooth. Add egg. Add flour and beat well. Add remaining 3-3 1/2 cups flour. Knead 5 minutes. Put in greased bowl until doubled, about 2 hours. Divide in half. Roll in balls and put in 9" x 13" pan, sprinkle with cinnamon mixture. Bake at 375 degrees for about 15 minutes or until light golden brown. (Can make the rolls plain or make into cinnamon rolls.)

Cinnamon Rolls

2 teaspoon cinnamon
3/4 cup brown sugar
1/2 cup raisins
1/2 cup nuts
confectioner's sugar frosting (optional)

Take half the dough, roll into large rectangle, spread with melted butter, sprinkle entire surface with cinnamon (about 2 teaspoons), sprinkle with brown sugar (about 3/4 cup), and roll up starting at long end. Press edge into dough. Cut into 1-inch (or size desired) pieces and place in 9" x 13" greased pan, edges touching. Bake at 375 degrees for 15-18 minutes, depending on size of rolls. You can frost if desired. You can also add nuts before rolling. Delicious!

—Nellie Huizenga

Apple Pastry Bars

2 1/2 cups flour
1 teaspoon salt
1 cup butter or shortening
1 egg, separated (keep both white and yolk)
milk to make 2/3 cup with egg yolk
2 handfuls corn flakes, crushed
9 apples
1 cup sugar
1 teaspoon cinnamon

Frosting
1 tablespoon water
1 cup confectioner's sugar
1 teaspoon vanilla

Combine flour and salt. Cut in shortening until crumbly. Combine egg yolk and milk to make 2/3 cup and add to flour mix all at once. Mix well. Roll out half of mixture and place in jelly roll pan (10" x 15" pan that looks like a cookie sheet with sides). Crumble two handfuls of corn flakes over top of crust.

Wash, core, and peel apples. Slice thin, and arrange on top of crust. Combine cinnamon and sugar and sprinkle over apples. Roll out remaining dough, and cover apples. Crimp edges. Beat egg white until almost stiff. Brush over top crust. Bake at 400 degrees for about 6 minutes. Combine frosting ingredients. Spread over slightly cooled crust. Cut into squares.

Sunday Night or
Picnic Supper

Cold Raspberry Soup
Greek Ravioli Pasta Salad
Avocado BLT Sandwich with Chive Cheese
on French Bread
Nestle's Crunch Ice Cream Dessert

Cold Raspberry Soup

2 ten-ounce packages of frozen raspberries (UNSWEETENED)
1 cup sugar
1/2 cup orange juice
1/4 cup lemon juice
1 tablespoon cornstarch
fresh orange sections from one orange, cut in pieces
1 cup raspberries, fresh

Puree defrosted raspberries through strainer. In saucepan, cook pureed raspberries, sugar, and juices. Add cornstarch; thicken until clear. Cool. Stir in fresh orange sections and fresh raspberries.

Greek Ravioli Pasta Salad

2 9-ounce packages cheese ravioli, cooked and drained
2 bunches asparagus, cooked and cut into 1-inch pieces (For this recipe I cut asparagus before cooking. If the asparagus has tough outer skin, peel with vegetable peeler.)
1 cup green onion, chopped
1 yellow squash, finely chopped
1 zucchini, chopped
8 ounces Feta cheese
4 ounces semi-hard cheese (such as Gruyere), grated
1 small can sliced black olives
6 diced tomatoes

Lemon Dressing (see American Menu, p. 121

Cook ravioli and drain. Mix all ingredients together, season with salt and pepper to taste. Chill. (Serves 8-10.)

Avocado BLT Sandwich with Chive Cheese on French Bread

1 pound bacon, cooked crisp, well drained, broken into small pieces
2 medium ripe tomatoes, sliced very thin
1 8-ounce package cream cheese, room temperature
1/4 cup snipped fresh chives, chopped
1/4 cup mayonnaise
1 package dry pesto mix
2 teaspoons lemon juice
4 drops hot sauce
2 ripe avocados
1/4 teaspoon salt
freshly ground pepper
Boston lettuce
1 loaf Italian bread

Chop bacon. Set aside. Slice tomatoes. Set aside. Combine cream cheese, chives, mayonnaise, pesto mix, 1 teaspoon lemon juice, and hot sauce. Beat until smooth and creamy.

To Assemble:
Split bread lengthwise, but do not cut through. Open carefully and hollow out loaf leaving 1/2 inch shell in each half. Spread cheese mixture over both sides. Sprinkle bottom half with bacon, patting gently into place. Peel and slice avocado. Toss with remaining lemon juice. Place on bread. Top with tomato slices. Sprinkle with salt and pepper. Arrange a single layer of shredded lettuce over tomatoes. Close sandwich and press together gently. To serve, cut loaf diagonally into wedges. You can also make in small individual loaves. Wrap in foil, to take to a picnic.

Nestle's Crunch Ice Cream Dessert

2 cups graham cracker crumbs
8 Nestle's Crunch candy bars, crumbled
4 tablespoons peanut butter
1 large jar maraschino cherries, drained and chopped
1 gallon ice cream, your choice

Mix crumbs, candy, peanut butter, and cherries together in large bowl or use processor and pulse until mixed into chunks and bits. DO NOT OVERMIX. YOU WILL HAVE MUSH!

Put half in bottom of 9" x 13" pan. Spread partially softened ice cream over, then remaining crumbs. Freeze.

(My friend Carol makes this recipe with chocolate cookie crumbs and Heath Bars.)

I like to have this on hand in the summer. When friends drop in, I have a wonderful treat for them. This is delicious!

Pork Dinner For Six

Squash and Apple Bisque
Herb-Crusted Pork Tenderloin with
Roasted Red Skins
Apple Sauté
Krenterbrood (Dutch Raisin Bread)
Banana Roll-up Cake with Fudge Sauce

Squash and Apple Bisque

2 packages frozen butternut squash, cooked
4 cups chicken stock (see "Begin with a Good Stock" on p. 121)
1 teaspoon cinnamon
1/4 teaspoon nutmeg
salt and pepper to taste
2 cups light cream
2 tablespoons sugar
1 large apple, cored and sliced
green onions, sliced for garnish
whipped cream or plain yogurt for garnish, optional

Place all ingredients except green onions and whipped cream in a large kettle. Simmer until thoroughly blended. (Do not boil.) Season to taste. Serve in a bowl or mug with dollop of whipped cream or yogurt, and a few pieces of green onion.

Herb–Crusted Pork Tenderloin with Roasted Red Skins

2 pounds red skin potatoes, medium size
1/4 cup butter, melted
2 tablespoons horseradish sauce
1 teaspoon salt
1/2 teaspoon pepper
1 1/2 cups bread crumbs (see p. 136 for directions)
1/3 cup fresh basil
1 tablespoon olive oil
1/2 teaspoon pepper
1 teaspoon salt
3 tablespoons fresh thyme, chopped
1 package pork tenderloins (2 per package)
3 tablespoons fresh parsley, chopped

Peel a one-inch strip around center of each potato. Place potatoes in large bowl. Add butter, horseradish sauce, salt, and pepper. Toss to coat potatoes. Place potatoes on a lightly greased rack in broiler pan. Bake at 425 degrees for 20 minutes.

Stir together bread crumbs, basil, pepper, salt, and thyme. Brush tenderloins lightly with olive oil. Roll in crumbs until completely covered. Roast at 425 degrees approximately 25 additional minutes until potatoes are tender and meat thermometer reaches 160 degrees when inserted in center of pork. Sprinkle with fresh chopped parsley, slice, and serve on platter with potatoes.

Apple Sauté

8 large apples (a mixture of Yellow Delicious and Granny Smith is good)
3 tablespoons butter
3 tablespoons honey
3 tablespoons brown sugar
dash salt
1/4 teaspoon nutmeg
1 teaspoon cinnamon

Melt butter in frying pan. Core and slice apples. Saute apples in butter over medium heat until softened. Add remaining ingredients, and cook approximately 5 minutes. Serve warm.

THIS IS A GREAT ACCOMPANIMENT TO ANY MEAT AND A NICE CHANGE FROM APPLESAUCE.

Krenterbrood (Dutch Raisin Bread)

1 tablespoon yeast
1/4 cup warm water
3/4 cup sugar
3/4 cup butter or margarine
1 1/2 cups warm milk
1 teaspoon salt
1 egg
1 1/2 cups raisins
1 1/2 cups currants
2 cups walnuts, coarsely chopped
6 cups flour (6-7 cups)

Microwave a bowl of hot water and soak raisins and other dried fruits until they absorb some of the water. Drain and dry fruit with paper toweling. Coarsely chop walnuts. Set aside.

Dissolve the yeast in warm water for about 10 minutes. Add other ingredients in order given. Save some flour for kneading dough. Dough should not be tough, but slightly sticky. Let rise until doubled. When doubled in size, punch down and shape into two loaves.

Let rise again (this will take longer to rise because of all the fruit). Bake until loaves are large and full. Bake at 375 for 40 minutes.

—Meg Huizenga

Banana Roll-up Cake with Fudge Sauce

1 stick butter or shortening
1 eight-ounce cream cheese, softened
1 three-ounce cream cheese, softened
1/2 cup sugar
1 egg
3 tablespoons milk
1/2 cup flour
1/2 teaspoon baking powder
1/4 teaspoon baking soda
4 eggs, separated into yolks and whites
1/2 teaspoon vanilla
1/3 cup sugar
1 large banana, mashed
1/2 cup finely chopped pecans

1/2 cup sugar
confectioner's sugar

Lightly grease 15" x 10" x 1" baking pan. Line bottom with wax paper and grease paper with butter or shortening. Set pan aside.

Filling

Combine cream cheeses and 1/2 cup sugar in a small mixing bowl. Beat with an electric mixer on medium speed until smooth. Add the egg and milk; beat until combined. Spread in prepared pan; set aside.

Cake

Combine flour, baking powder, and baking soda in a medium bowl. Beat egg yolks and vanilla in a small bowl with an electric mixer on medium speed about five minutes, or until thick and lemon colored. Gradually add the 1/3 cup sugar, beating until sugar is dissolved. Stir in banana and nuts.

Thoroughly wash beaters. Beat egg whites in a large mixing bowl with an electric mixer on medium speed until soft peaks form. Gradually add 1/2 cup sugar, beating on high speed until stiff peaks form. Fold egg yolk mixture into egg white mixture. Sprinkle flour mixture evenly over egg mixture; fold in just until combined. Carefully spread batter evenly over filling in pan. Be careful not to dig into cream cheese mixture.

Bake in 375-degree oven for 15-20 minutes or until the cake springs back when lightly touched. Immediately loosen cake from sides of pan and turn out onto a towel sprinkled with powdered sugar.

Carefully peel off paper. Starting with a short side, roll up cake using towel to support cake as you roll it (this keeps the cake from cracking). Cool completely on a wire rack.

To serve, place a small amount of chocolate sauce under slice of cake. Sprinkle with confectioner's sugar. If chocolate is too thick, add a small amount of milk.

Fudge Sauce (Low Fat)

1 can sweetened condensed milk, fat free
2 squares unsweetened chocolate
1 teaspoon vanilla

Pour sweetened condensed milk into small saucepan. Add chocolate, and stir over low heat until completely blended. Cool. Add vanilla.

Chinese Dinner

Hot Sour Soup
Egg Rolls with Shrimp and Pork
Delicious Pepper Steak with Oyster Sauce
Coconut Pound Cake

Hot Sour Soup

Sauce
1 1/2 tablespoons cornstarch, mixed with 2 tablespoons water
1 tablespoon vinegar
1/2 teaspoon pepper
1/2 teaspoon Tabasco sauce
Salt, to taste

Combine ingredients, stirring until cornstarch dissolves.

Main Recipe
4 mushrooms
3 green onions
3/4 cup sliced ham
5 cups chicken stock (see "Begin with a Good Stock" on p. 121)
1/4 cup shredded bamboo shoots
12 shrimp, shelled (cooked or uncooked)
3 eggs, uncooked, beaten
1 package frozen snow peas, cut into thin strips

Cut mushrooms, onion, and ham into very thin strips. Bring chicken stock to boil and add mushrooms, onion, ham, and bamboo shoots. Cook for about 3 minutes. Add shrimp and sauce; cook for 2 additional minutes. Stir in beaten eggs. Add snow peas. Cook 1-2 minutes more. (Serves 8.)

Egg Rolls with Shrimp and Pork

1 package egg roll skins
1 egg, lightly beaten

Filling

1/2 pound cooked shrimp, cut into small bits
1 tablespoon soy sauce
1 teaspoon salt
1 teaspoon sugar
1 tablespoon white grape juice
1/2 teaspoon cornstarch
1 can bean sprouts, drained
1/2 pound fresh, lean boneless ground pork
4 cups celery, fine dice
1 tablespoon cornstarch in 2 tablespoons chicken stock (see "Begin with a Good Stock" on p. 121)
3 tablespoons oil
1 teaspoon salt
1/2 teaspoon sugar
1/3 cup mushrooms, finely chopped
oil for deep frying

Mix shrimp in a bowl with soy sauce, 1 teaspoon salt, 1 teaspoon sugar, grape juice, and cornstarch. Drain bean sprouts and rinse in cold water 2 or 3 times.

Heat 1 tablespoon oil in a frying pan over medium flame and cook shrimp mixture for about 3 minutes. Place in dish and set aside. In same pan, heat 1 tablespoon oil over high flame and add pork. Stir fry for 2 minutes, or until it loses its reddish color. Set aside.

In a clean frying pan, heat 1 tablespoon oil and add celery. Stir rapidly over high flame for about two minutes. Add pork. Add salt, and 1/2 teaspoon sugar; mix well. Cook for 5 minutes over medium flame. Add mushrooms and mix thoroughly. Then add sprouts and mix a few times. Lastly, add the shrimp, and add the cornstarch-and-chicken-stock mixture. Cook until thickened. Cool thoroughly before using as filling.

How to Wrap Egg Roll:

For each egg roll, shape about 1/4 cup of filling with your hands into a cylinder about four inches long and an inch in diameter, and place it diagonally across the center of a wrapper. Lift the lower triangular flap over the filling and tuck the point under it, leaving the upper point of the wrapper exposed. Bring each of the two small end flaps, one at a time, up to the top of the enclosed filling and press the points firmly down. Brush the upper and exposed triangle of dough with the lightly beaten egg, and then roll the wrapper into a neat package. The beaten egg will seal the edges and keep the wrapper intact. (See diagram.)

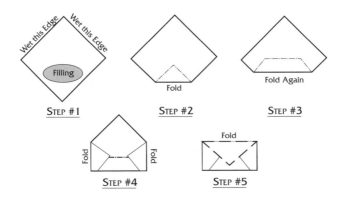

Cooking Procedure:

Heat oil to 375 degrees and deep fry the egg rolls one at a time for 3-5 minutes, until each is golden brown. Remove with metal slotted spoon. Drain on paper towels. Serve hot with mustard, sweet and sour sauce, and/or soy sauce.

Makes 18 egg rolls. These take time, but if you make the filling ahead, they are well worth the effort. This mixture will keep overnight, but keep very cold in airtight container.

(Note to Cooking Mentor: It is fun for each woman to roll her own egg roll and to fry it to know just how it should be done.)

Delicious Pepper Steak with Oyster Sauce

Don't be afraid of the oyster sauce. It has a lovely, delicate flavor. I love it, and I don't eat oysters!

1 pound flank steak, sliced as thin as possible
2 tablespoons soy sauce
1 1/2 teaspoons cornstarch
1 tablespoon white grape juice
1 teaspoon sugar
1/2 teaspoon ginger
4 tablespoons cooking oil
2 green peppers
1 teaspoon salt

Freeze meat slightly. This makes it easy to slice thinly! Cut the beef across the grain in thin 1/4-inch slices or thinner. I like to shave it as thinly as possible with a very sharp knife. Mix sliced beef with soy sauce, cornstarch, juice, and sugar. Set aside. (This part of the recipe can be done the night before. Keep meat in an airtight bag or container.)

Rinse green pepper, then cut in thin, lengthwise strips and discard seeds and trim off white soft parts of the inside of pepper.

Sauce

4 tablespoons beef or chicken stock (see "Begin with a Good Stock" on p. 121)
1/2 teaspoon salt
1 teaspoon sugar
1 teaspoon sesame oil
2 tablespoons bottled oyster sauce
Pinch pepper
1 teaspoon cornstarch

Combine ingredients, stirring until cornstarch dissolves.

Cooking Procedure:

Heat the oil in hot skillet or wok over a high heat. Add salt first and green pepper, stirring constantly until the pepper turns darker green (about a minute or two). Remove green pepper and spread out on a plate. In the same skillet, add the remaining 2 tablespoons oil and ginger, stir in beef mixture, and turn constantly until the beef is almost cooked (about 2-3 minutes).

Add green pepper and mix well. Stir in the sauce mixture. It will thicken gradually. When the steak is thoroughly mixed with the sauce, serve as soon as possible.

Rice:

I like Uncle Ben's Long Grain Rice, and I follow the quantities and directions on the box. Rice-a-Roni makes a very nice fried rice recipe.

Coconut Pound Cake

1 cup butter, softened
3 cups sugar
6 eggs
3 cups flour
1/4 teaspoon baking soda
1/4 teaspoon salt
1 cup sour cream
1 cup coconut
1 teaspoon vanilla
1 teaspoon coconut extract
1/4 cup confectioner's sugar (as a garnish)
1 pint whipping cream, whipped
fresh fruit (optional)

Grease and flour a tube pan (angelfood cake pan). Cream butter and sugar until light and fluffy. Add eggs one at a time. Mix flour, soda, and salt. Add flour mixture to creamed mixture alternately with sour cream. Stir in coconut, coconut extract, and vanilla.

Bake at 350 degrees for 1 hour and 20 minutes in tube pan. Test at one hour and 10 minutes. Do not overbake. Cool in pan. Remove carefully to cake plate. Serve sprinkled with confectioner's sugar and a dollop of whipped cream! Add fresh fruit, such as peaches, if you like.

Baked Chicken Dinner

Parmesan Chicken
Roasted Tomatoes
Onion-Gruyere Tart
Quick and Easy Popovers
Meringue Clouds with Berries

Parmesan Chicken

2 sticks butter
3/4 cup fresh breadcrumbs (see below for directions)
1/3 cup Parmesan cheese, grated
1 1/2 tablespoons Italian seasoning
1 teaspoon garlic, crushed
1/4 teaspoon salt
1/4 teaspoon pepper
3 whole skinless chicken breasts, split
1/4 cup white grape juice
1/4 cup green onion, chopped
1/4 cup parsley, chopped

Preheat oven to 375 degrees. Divide butter in two parts. Melt one part of butter. In a small bowl, combine bread crumbs, cheese, and Italian seasoning. Dip chicken in butter, then roll in crumbs. Place on a broiler pan. Bake for 25 minutes. Combine juice, onion, and parsley with remaining butter. Pour over chicken. Cook for five minutes more. (Serves 6.) BE SURE TO USE FRESH BUTTER IN SAUCE, SO THAT BUTTER IS NOT CONTAMINATED BY RAW CHICKEN.

Fresh Breadcrumbs

Make fresh breadcrumbs from dry bread with your food processor. Keep in air-tight container or bag in freezer. You can use leftover rolls and bread of any kind. This is a real savings.

Roasted Tomatoes

PICK THE RIPEST, MEATIEST TOMATOES AVAILABLE FOR THE BEST FLAVOR.

8 sliced tomatoes (3/4-inch thick or more)
olive oil
2 tablespoons sugar
1 teaspoon salt
dash pepper
Herbs de Provence or Italian seasoning

Slice tomatoes, and place on greased cookie sheet. Brush with olive oil. Mix together sugar, salt, and dash pepper. Sprinkle over top. Sprinkle herbs over top. Bake at 250 for three hours. (YES! THREE HOURS.)

—Nancy Gerhard

Onion–Gruyere Tart

2 tablespoons butter
3 large onions, thinly sliced
prepared refrigerated pie crust
2 cups Gruyere cheese, grated
1 tablespoon all-purpose flour
1 teaspoon fresh thyme, chopped
1/2 teaspoon salt
1/4 teaspoon nutmeg
1/4 teaspoon white pepper
2 eggs, room temperature
1/2 cup half and half

In large skillet, over medium heat, melt butter. Cook onions until very soft and golden, stirring occasionally. (Pick the sweetest onions you can find, such as Vidalia.)

Preheat oven to 425 degrees. Gently press crust onto bottom and sides of an 11" tart pan with removable bottom. Arrange Gruyere cheese in pan; sprinkle flour, thyme, salt, nutmeg, and white pepper over top. Toss lightly to combine; smooth top to make an even layer. Add cooked onions, arranging evenly. In small bowl, whisk together eggs and half and half; pour evenly over onions and cheese mixture.

Place tart on cookie sheet; bake 10 minutes. Reduce oven temperature to 375 degrees, and bake 20 minutes longer, or until filling is puffy and set.

Cool slightly before serving. Or cool tart completely, cover, and refrigerate. Reheat at 350 degrees before serving. (Serves 10.)

—Nancy Gerhard

Quick and Easy Popovers

2 eggs
1/4 teaspoon salt
1 cup milk
2 tablespoons butter, melted
1 cup flour

Butter 12 standard-size muffin cups or a popover pan.

In a bowl, combine eggs and salt. Using a whisk, beat lightly. Stir in milk and butter and beat in the flour just until blended. Do not over beat. Fill each cup about half full and place in cold oven. Set temperature to 425 and bake for 20 minutes. Reduce heat to 375 and bake until the popovers are golden, 10-15 minutes longer. They should be crisp on the outside. Quickly pierce each popover with a thin metal skewer or the tip of a small knife to release the steam. Leave in the oven a couple of minutes for further crisping. Remove and serve at once. Makes 12 muffins or 6 popovers.

Serve with fruit or honey-flavored butter. Make honey butter by adding 1 tablespoon honey to 1/2 cup softened butter. Cream together until thoroughly blended.

Meringue Clouds with Berries

6 egg whites
1/4 teaspoon salt
3/4 teaspoon cream of tartar
1 1/2 cups sugar
1 cup Marscarpone cheese (or 1 8-ounce cream cheese)
1 cup sugar
1 teaspoon vanilla
2 cups whipping cream, whipped
2 cups miniature marshmallows

Heat oven to 375 degrees. Spread cookie sheet with parchment paper. Beat room-temperature egg whites, cream of tartar, and salt until frothy. Gradually add 1 1/2 cups of sugar. Beat until stiff and glossy. Drop by large spoon (about 1/2 cup each) onto cookie sheet. Make approximately 12.

With back of spoon, swirl a hole in center, being careful to keep a nice, round

mound. Put into oven, turn oven off and leave until dried and cooled, about 12 hours or overnight. Do not peek. Keep oven door closed until ready to use. It is very important to keep meringues dry.

Mix Marscarpone cheese with 1 cup sugar and vanilla. Fold in whipping cream and marshmallows. Spread evenly among meringues.

Topping
1 cup fresh sliced strawberries
1 cup fresh raspberries
1/2-3/4 cup sugar

Mix strawberries and raspberries with 1/2 cup sugar. Let set until some juice is drawn from fruit. Serve over meringues.

For Further Reading

The following are some basic recipe books I often recommend:

Nicole Routhier, *The Fruit Cookbook* (New York: Workman Publishing, 1996).

Flo Braker, *The Simple Art of Perfect Baking* (Shelburne, Vt.: Chapters Publishing, Ltd., 1992).

Anne Willan, *La Varenne Pratique* (New York: Crown Publishers, Inc., 1989).

Bonnie Stewart Mickelson, *Hollyhocks and Radishes: A Mrs. Chard's Almanac Cookbook* (Bellevue, Wash.: Pickle Point Publishing, 1989).

You can reach Betty Huizenga through the Apples of Gold Web site: www.applesofgold.org.

The Songs

Apples of Gold

Betty Huizenga

Kindness

Betty Huizenga

Loving Your Husband

Betty Huizenga

A Mother's Prayer

Betty Huizenga

Submission

Betty Huizenga

Purity

Betty Huizenga

Hospitality

Betty Huizenga

Mentor's Covenant

1. I covenant that I have accepted Jesus Christ as my Lord and Savior, and seek to honor him in my life.

2. I will seek to be a servant of the Lord in the progream of Apples of Gold, having the interests of the younger women in my heart.

3. I will prepare the lessons ahead of time, both the one I teach and the other lessons.

4. I will faithfully pray for the Apples of Gold program and for each participant.

5. I will, as best I can, befriend each woman in the class and make myself available to her.

6. I will attend all six classes, the "Applesauce" meetings, and the final dinner with spouses, Lord willing. If I am unable to attend a class, I will clear my absence with the other mentors.

Mentor's signature _____

Date _____

Participant's Covenant

1. I will be a faithful participant in the Apples of Gold classes, not missing more than one lesson.

2. I will pray for the ministry of Apples of Gold, including each mentor and each woman in my class.

3. I will prepare each lesson in advance, asking the Lord to give me wisdom and insight, and a heart open to obey what He shows me in the lesson and class.

4. I desire to serve the Lord and my family through the lessons learned at Apples of Gold.

Signature _____

Date _____